Cambridge Discovery Readers

Level 6

Series editor: Nicholas Tims

Freddie's War

Jane Rollason

CAMBRIDGE
UNIVERSITY PRESS

CAMBRIDGE UNIVERSITY PRESS

Cambridge, New York, Melbourne, Madrid, Cape Town,
Singapore, São Paulo, Delhi, Tokyo, Mexico City

Cambridge University Press
79 Anson Road, #06-04/06, Singapore 079906

www.cambridge.org

This American English edition is based on *Freddie's War* ISBN 978-84-8323-909-4
first published by Cambridge University Press in 2010.

First published 2010
American English edition 2011

Printed in Singapore by NPE Print Communications Pte Ltd

ISBN 978-0-521-18160-0 Paperback American English edition

Illustrations by Jordi Solano

Exercises by Jane Rollason

Contents

People in the story

Freddie Fox: 17, from Middleton, Yorkshire, England
Laura Marcos: 17, lives in Badajoz, Spain
Alonso Marcos: 19, Laura's brother
Javier Marcos: Laura and Alonso's father
Ruben Sosa: Laura and Alonso's uncle
Isabel Marcos de Sosa: Laura and Alonso's aunt
Ray: 23, an American in Europe

BEFORE YOU READ
• •

1 Look at the cover and *People in the story*. Answer the questions.

1 Who do you think the person on the train is?

2 Do you think this story takes place now or in the past?

Prologue

Who's who in *Freddie's War*

This story starts in Yorkshire in the north of England and then moves to Spain. The story happens during the civil war in Spain, which started on July 17, 1936, and lasted for three years. The Second World War started exactly six months after the civil war ended.

The Republicans: Spain had become a Republic in 1931, and the Republicans were the democratically[1] elected government side. The Soviet Union sent soldiers and weapons to help the Spanish government, in return for Spanish gold. Britain and France did not want to join the war, and they refused to help the Spanish government. However, thousands of volunteers from countries around the world, including Britain, France, and the United States, did want to help. They went to Spain as volunteers, and many were formed into the International Brigades.

The Nationalists: This was the rebel side. General Franco was leader of the Nationalists, and he led Spain's Army of Africa, based in Morocco, to overthrow the democratically elected Republican government. He was sent planes and soldiers by Hitler in Germany and Mussolini in Italy. Franco wanted to bring back the traditional and conservative way of life that had existed in Spain before the Republic.

Chapter 1

Get me out!

Yorkshire, England, July 1936

Freddie closed the metal gate and shut his eyes tight. The elevator began its high-speed journey underground. It took seven seconds to reach the bottom.

"One, two, three . . ." Freddie counted. The elevator shook as it came to a stop. But Freddie had only got to five. He opened his eyes. He saw only black walls. He started to panic. His body began to sweat and shake. His mouth was dry.

"Hey!" he shouted into the blackness. "The elevator's stuck. Get me out!"

A few more seconds passed.

Suddenly the elevator shook again and down it went.

At the bottom, Freddie pushed open the door and fell out into the heat and dust of the mine.

"Look who it is stuck in the elevator!" laughed a voice, "Freddie Fox!"

The voice belonged to Ralph. Ralph was the same age as Freddie, and they had been in the same class at school.

"Were you scared, Freddie? You're worse than my little sister," Ralph added.

Freddie breathed deeply. "I'm looking for the boss," he said. "I've got a message for him."

"That way," said Ralph, pointing down one of the tunnels. Freddie ran off, his face burning in shame.

SPAIN: CIVIL WAR BREAKS OUT
—
Hitler Sends Planes to Help Franco

When Freddie got home from work, his father was putting coal into the fire in the tiny kitchen. Supper was cooking on top, and the air in the room was hot and thick. Freddie made some tea. Freddie's dad sat on a low chair next to the fire, his back bent. Freddie stared out of the window. They didn't speak.

Freddie took his tea through to the living room. His mother sat at the table, writing.

"How was work?" she asked.

"The same as usual," said Freddie. He took a newspaper out of his pocket and handed it to her.

"Oh, thanks," she said. "What's happening in the world today? *'German planes arrived in Morocco yesterday,'*" she read aloud, "*'to transport soldiers from Spanish bases in north Africa across to mainland Spain this week. Mr. Hitler has promised to help the Spanish Army of Africa –'*"

"Do you think there's going to be a war here in England?" asked Freddie.

"Yes, I'm afraid there is. The war could easily spread to other countries, especially now that Germany is getting involved," said his mother. "What a terrible thought!"

"Maybe I should go to Spain," said Freddie. "It says in the paper that people are volunteering from all over the world –"

"Men, not boys," said Freddie's father, coming into the room. "You need to stay here and help put food on this table."

Freddie's mom went to get the dinner. She called Freddie's brothers and sister, and the family squeezed around the table. There was barely room to lift their knives and forks.

"If I was Freddie, I'd go to Spain," said his mom.

"Don't encourage him," said his father.

"I don't have to fight," said Freddie. "I could work for a newspaper and send money home."

"You could write reports from the front line. And Freddie and I have been learning Spanish," said his mom. "I'd definitely go if I had the chance."

"Not that writing nonsense again," said Freddie's dad. "You should get down that mine and earn a proper day's money."

"You know he can't go down the mine," said his mom.

"How can he go to war then?" said his dad. "I know what war's like. It's no place for a soft boy like Freddie. Now let me eat my dinner in peace."

After dinner, Freddie walked up the hill overlooking the mining town of Middleton. The heat of the day hung in the evening air. Some others who worked down the mine were there. They kicked a ball around for a while and then played cards.

Even though everyone washed after work, they still looked dirty. Lines of coal dust ringed their faces. It was a mining town, and for the young men there was only one path. When you left school, you took a job underground, just like your father. Except Freddie, who worked above ground. His face was clean.

Freddie had been a bit of a joke at school. He didn't like playing tricks on the teacher or fighting in the playground. When the teams were chosen for a game of soccer, Freddie was always picked last.

When they all left school, he'd gone to work down the mine with the rest of them. But his problems started on the first day. His body started to panic as soon as he stepped into the elevator. He was always sweating and shaking by the time it arrived. The first few times, his father shouted at him and his friends laughed. But that didn't help, and the sweating and shaking got worse. So he was given a job in the office. He was smart, after all, and he was good at writing letters. Most days, however, he still had to take messages down into the mine, which he hated.

The young men lay around on the grass with nothing to do. Ralph was there. He told the others about Freddie getting stuck in the elevator. "Typical Freddie," they said.

Freddie tried to change the subject. "Looks like there's a war starting in Spain," he said.

"Spain?" said Ralph. "Where's Spain?"

"It's next to France," said Freddie.

Ralph rolled onto his elbows and looked at Freddie.

"I know where Spain is, you fool," said Ralph. "But I don't care, see?"

"Maybe we should go and fight, that's all," said Freddie.

"I can just see you in the army, Freddie," said one of the others. "You'll have your hands in the air before the enemy's got his gun out."

They all laughed.

"Why would we fight someone else's war, anyway?" said Ralph. "If it's fighting you want, you can fight me."

Freddie looked over the town toward the horizon.

"I fancy that sister of yours," said Ralph to Freddie, after a while. The others laughed and whistled.

"You keep your hands off my sister," said Freddie.

"Ooh! I'm scared," said Ralph. The others laughed.

Freddie threw himself at Ralph, and they rolled down the slope, hitting out with their fists. "Fight! Fight!" shouted the others, jumping up and circling around. Within seconds, Ralph was holding Freddie down on the hard ground. He raised his fist, ready to punch.

"Leave it, Ralph," said one of the others. "Let him go."

Ralph slowly got off Freddie, his arm still raised. Freddie got to his feet and walked down toward the railway line. He couldn't hear the laughter anymore, but he could still feel it.

* * *

The next day, Freddie had to take the safety report book down into the mine. The elevator traveled smoothly this time, and Freddie ran along the tunnel, looking for Mr. Taylor, the boss. He passed two miners on their way to the elevator.

"Any sign of the boss?" he called.

"He's further along the tunnel," one of them shouted back, "where the new tunnel starts."

Freddie didn't usually go this far into the mine. Sweat was running down his face, and his heart was beating fast.

Mr. Taylor was looking up at the roof in the new tunnel when Freddie found him. There was a miner with him – Ralph! Freddie handed over the report book.

"Freddie! Two visits in two days! You'll be wanting a job down here next!" joked Ralph.

But then Ralph stopped laughing. There was a cracking noise above their heads. They all looked up. Suddenly a cloud of dust burst from the roof of the tunnel.

"Run!" shouted Ralph. Freddie and Ralph ran back into the old tunnel. Big rocks crashed down behind them in the new tunnel. They heard Mr. Taylor scream. Dust filled the tunnel. They couldn't see. Freddie stopped and felt the panic rising through his body. The boss screamed again.

"Come on," cried Ralph. "Run!"

"Wh-What about the boss?" shouted Freddie.

"Leave him," said Ralph.

"No, we can't," said Freddie. For a second, Freddie just stood where he was. It felt like an hour. His body wanted to run, but he couldn't leave the boss. He went blindly back into the new tunnel and found the boss lying on the floor.

"Mr. Taylor?" he shouted. "Are you alive?"

"Freddie," groaned the boss. "H-Help me. Don't leave me . . . my leg . . ."

"You'll be OK. We'll get you out," Freddie said, not believing his own words. The dust was clearing now, and he could see that the boss's leg was trapped under a rock. He tried to pull him out.

"Ralph!" he called. "Help me. We've got to move this rock."

Ralph was close behind him.

"I'm not waiting," said Ralph. "I'm getting out of here."

Just at that moment, there was another dreadful crack and a new fall of rock. This time it was on the other side of them, in the old tunnel. Dust blinded them again.

"No!" screamed Ralph. "Freddie, you fool. We're trapped. Now we'll never get out." His voice rose in terror. He felt his way to the new rock fall and began to pull wildly at the lumps of rock.

Freddie took short breaths. He crawled into the old tunnel and away from the rock fall, deeper into the mine where there was more air. He sat with his back to the wall. He shut his eyes and counted, trying to breathe air into his lungs.

They could see light at the top of the rock fall. Freddie went back to the boss.

"Mr. Taylor?" he said.

"Freddie, help me," groaned Mr. Taylor.

"Leave him," cried Ralph. "Help! Help!"

Freddie ignored Ralph and tried to free the boss's leg. Mr. Taylor carried a hammer on his belt, and Freddie used it to break up the lumps of rock that were holding his foot. Freddie worked patiently. Concentrating on the task helped him forget his fear. After a while, he was able to loosen the boss's thick boot and gently pull his foot out.

"Give me a hand, Ralph," Freddie called. "He's free. Help me move him."

Ralph wasn't listening. "We're going to die," he was saying over and over again.

Freddie took hold of the boss under his arms and dragged him into the old tunnel. He laid him down carefully.

Ralph turned on Freddie. "This is your fault," he said. "If we'd run when I said, we'd be out of here. Why did you go back for him? He'll probably die anyway."

"Shut up, Ralph, he'll hear you," said Freddie.

"Freddie . . ." whispered Mr. Taylor. "Thank you . . . I'll never forget this." And then his head fell to the side. Freddie put his cheek to the man's mouth.

"He's still breathing," said Freddie. "But I think he's unconscious."

"Who cares?" said Ralph. "We're all going to die now anyway."

"Ssh! Listen," said Freddie. "Someone's calling."

"Hello," came a voice from the other side of the fall.

"We're here," screamed Ralph. "Get us out!"

*   *   *

Some hours later, Ralph and Freddie stepped out of the elevator into the daylight. Their parents and their friends were all there. The rescuers carried Mr. Taylor out. A reporter from the local newspaper stepped forward and spoke to Freddie.

"Congratulations," he said. "You saved your boss's life. Tell us what happened." Ralph pushed in front of Freddie and smiled.

"We're lucky to be alive," he said. "Just after I got the boss clear of the new tunnel, more of the roof came down. The boss and I would have been killed. Freddie just wanted to get out, but I couldn't leave another man, a miner, to die."

A great cheer went up.

"Good man, Ralph!" someone shouted.

"But – ow!" said Freddie.

Ralph had his hand around Freddie's arm and he squeezed it hard.

"That's the way it was, right?" Ralph whispered in Freddie's ear, a twisted smile on his face.

Freddie tried to stand up for himself.

"Ralph, you know that's not what happened –" he started to say, but nobody was listening. And who would believe him anyway?

The miners lifted Ralph onto their shoulders and carried him off down the street. Everyone ran after them, shouting and clapping.

Freddie turned away. His mother and father were standing there, looking at him.

Freddie saw that his father was ashamed.

"Dad!" said Freddie. "It wasn't like Ralph said . . ." But his dad had already turned away.

"It wasn't like that, Mum," said Freddie. "Ralph wanted to leave the boss, not me."

"I believe you, Freddie," she said and hugged her son.

"But Dad doesn't believe me," said Freddie, "and no one else will."

* * *

The next day at work, nobody spoke to Freddie. The office workers and the miners all ignored him. When he went into the local shop after work, everyone stopped speaking. Even his family were cold, apart from his mother.

After supper, he sat on his bed and looked at the newspaper. Ralph's face stared at him from the front page. "*Hero Saves Mine Boss*," it said. "*Mr. Taylor is in a coma . . . he may remain unconscious for some time*," Freddie read, "*but doctors say he will live*." Freddie opened the paper and read about the war in Spain. He tried to imagine what it was like, how different it was from this cold, dark mining town where everything was covered in dust and everyone thought he was a coward. Suddenly his future was clear. He would go to Spain and fight General Franco and the fascists[2]. Nobody would know anything about him there. He would start again.

He packed a few things into a backpack. He laid out his work suit and his Sunday shoes. Then he climbed into bed and stared at the coal-black ceiling.

At dawn the next morning, Freddie waited by the railway line. The morning coal train was in Middleton station, about to start its journey to London. Freddie was hiding on the bank behind some bushes, out of sight of the train driver.

He heard the engine building up power. The wheels started to turn, and the train moved slowly out of the station.

"Now or never," said Freddie.

Freddie ran down the bank and jumped onto the side of the last carriage. He hung on tight and climbed inside.

The train was picking up speed now. Around the corner it passed under a footbridge. Someone was there, waving. It was his mother! Freddie waved back wildly.

"I'll write," he shouted, and laughed out loud.

Chapter 2

We must fight for Spain

Badajoz, Spain, August 1936

From the walls of the castle, Laura looked down to the river that was flowing lazily past the town. In the heat of the afternoon, it was the only thing moving. Even up here, there was no wind.

She started to walk down toward the river when she noticed something in the water. At first she thought it was someone swimming. Then she realized that it was a body. It floated gently with the current.

Laura had seen dead bodies before. Five years ago, she had seen her own mother lying dead in bed after her long illness. And she'd seen lots of dead animals, of course. But never a stranger, like this, just floating.

Laura became aware of a distant sound and climbed back up to the castle to see what it was. She saw a tiny insectlike thing in the sky, approaching the town. As it came closer, she dropped down behind a wall. The noise rushed over her head, as the small plane came in low over the castle. It circled above the town, spying.

As she ran home, she passed groups of people in the streets. Their faces were tense; their voices were sharp and afraid. Some of the older women were crying, with their hands over their ears.

Laura ran up the steps into her house.

"Father!" she called. She found her father, Señor Marcos, in his study. Her brother Alonso was there, too.

"Laura!" said her father. "Where have you been? You must stay in the house – it isn't safe outside."

"Father!" she said, "I saw a body – in the river – just below the castle, and then a plane came over."

Señor Marcos put his arms around his daughter.

"The Nationalists have taken control of Mérida," he said, "and we're cut off from the rest of the country."

"Do you think we can hold the Nationalists off?" said Laura.

"I'm sure we can," he said. "There are thousands of Republican soldiers here in Badajoz. They'll defend us."

Later, the family ate supper in the kitchen.

"I don't know what's happened to this town," said the housekeeper. "At the market this morning, one of our neighbors pushed me out of the way, like a stranger. She didn't even say sorry."

"Everyone is afraid," said Señor Marcos. "They don't know who will betray them."

"People will think we're on the fascist side," said Laura. "We're rich, we have a big house, our brother Esteban is in the Nationalist army, and Father employs half the town."

"Everyone knows Father," said Alonso. "They know he's a fair man. They know he believes in the government and the Republic – he would never support Franco and the Nationalist rebels."

"There are plenty of people who want the fascists to win, Alonso," said Señor Marcos. "And I have plenty of enemies."

"Father, if the Nationalists win, they'll kill you," said Laura. "You must go to Portugal. You can come back when it's safe."

"And what about you?" said her father, smiling. "Are you going to stay here and fight the rebels?"

"Of course," said Laura. "This is our war. We must fight it. And lots of women are fighting for the Republic. This war is a chance for women to stand alongside men."

"Laura, you're too young to fight. You're only just 17!" said her father.

Kaboom! Glass showered across the table as the windows at the end of the room exploded. Plates and dishes flew off the table and smashed on the stone floor. Everyone rocked on their chairs as their world was blown apart.

"Agh!" cried Señor Marcos.

"Father, are you hurt?" shouted Laura.

"Heaven save us!" cried the housekeeper, coughing as clouds of dust filled the room.

They all fell to the floor as there was a second explosion in the garden.

* * *

One evening, a few days later, Laura and Alonso's father called them into the study. Bags of sand were piled up in front of the windows, and their father lay on the sofa with his leg in bandages. A piece of metal from the first explosion had cut through his ankle.

"Laura! Alonso! Come here!" he said. "You must leave now. The mayor has just been to see me with the latest news. The Republicans are still in control of this part of town, but by morning, it will be over. The fighting is getting closer and closer to the house. Go to Portugal – there's still time, but you must go now, and you must only travel at night. Follow the river."

They heard gunfire through the broken windows.

"We can't leave you, Father," said Laura. "We will fight here and die with you."

"Laura's right, Father," said Alonso.

"I'm not going to die," said Señor Marcos. "They may take me prisoner, but I can survive that. We will be together again when all this is over. Remember that your mother's brother is in Saint Jean de Luz, in France, just over the border. He's the British Consul[3] there. You can always go to him for help."

Laura put her arms around her father and cried silently.

"Now look," he said, taking a letter from his pocket. "Take this letter – it's from Esteban. It says who you are – his brother and sister – and you mustn't be harmed. He sent it to me last week from Seville. It may save your lives if the Nationalists capture you."

"Come with us, Father," said Alonso. "We can help you."

"Alonso, I cannot even walk across the room. Now, please, kiss me and go. Look after your sister and stay alive."

An hour later, Laura and her brother were in the garden. They kept low behind the garden wall at the back of their house. There was no moon, and they wore dark clothes. They looked across the lawn toward the trees.

"Let's wait until it's really dark," whispered Alonso.

"Alonso," Laura whispered back, "I'm not going to Portugal."

"Are you crazy?" said Alonso. "Father said –"

"We can't leave Spain," said Laura. "This is our country – we must fight for it."

"But what can we do – you and me?" said Alonso.

"We can get to the Republican zone and –"

"Ssh!" said Alonso.

They both dropped down flat. Men in rebel uniforms ran along the road past their house, carrying guns.

The darkness had deepened now, and they started to creep toward the trees. When shouts from the street broke the silence, they stood up and ran across the lawn. Nobody saw them, and they carried on toward the river. They had lived on this land all their lives, and they could move quickly in the dark.

"So what do you think?" hissed Laura when they reached the riverbank. "Are you coming with me?"

"Well, I'm not letting you go on your own!" said Alonso. "Of course I'm coming with you. And you're right. We must fight for Spain."

"Yes!" said Laura, and she kissed her brother. "Of course I'm right . . . so, shall we take the boat?"

"Let's swim," said Alonso. "The boat's too risky."

Holding their bags above their heads, Laura and Alonso walked silently into the black water. It hadn't rained all summer, and the river was very low. They reached the opposite bank and lay in the water, listening.

"OK, let's go," whispered Alonso. They pulled themselves out of the river. There was a sudden noise very near them – a branch breaking. They froze . . . until they saw the green eyes of a fox looking at them.

In the next few hours, Laura and Alonso covered a lot of ground. First, they circled around the north of Badajoz and then headed east. The town shone out in the dark as buildings burned. Bombs exploded in the sky like fireworks, and there was a terrible smell in the air.

They knew the river system well and kept alongside waterways. When daylight came, they hid in thick woodland. Taking turns to sleep, the hours passed quickly. From time to time, they heard a plane or a distant explosion. The battle for Badajoz wasn't over yet. As the light began to fade, they faced up to their future.

"Where shall we go?" said Laura.

"Let's think about our options first. Do you really want to put yourself in danger? We could still give ourselves up to the Nationalists," said Alonso. "After all, we've got Esteban's letter to show them."

"Never!" said Laura. "Anyway, they might kill us before they see it."

"It's just that Dad told me to look after you and take you to Portugal," said Alonso. "Twenty-four hours later, I'm doing exactly the opposite."

"You can blame me," said Laura, smiling.

"But think about it, Laura," said Alonso. "Spain will still be run by Spaniards if the rebels win – it's not like an invasion."

"Alonso," said Laura. "These people aren't interested in a free, modern Spain like we want. They don't want progress. They want to go back to the old ways, where the church controls everything, women don't have opinions, workers don't ask questions –"

"OK, OK," said Alonso. "Spare me the speech! Whatever we do, we must keep away from Mérida or any place where the rebels are in control," said Alonso. "We could try and get to Uncle Ruben and Aunt Isabel's. What do you think?"

"Yes, good idea. Their farm is a long way from the town. Why would the Nationalists bother with them? At least we know we'll be welcome there."

"And we could stay there until it's over," said Alonso, "it may only be a few days or weeks."

They traveled east, moving fast over the flat land. This time, they didn't stop when daylight came, and by the end of the next day, they had reached the woods behind their uncle and aunt's farmhouse. That night, they slept on beds of leaves, dreaming about their aunt's cooking. The next morning, they woke early and waited for signs of life in the farmhouse.

The English Channel, August 1936

Freddie stood on deck and watched England disappear. He had never seen the sea before or even been on a boat. The sea was calm, and people sat on benches, enjoying the sun. There were plenty of young men on the crossing. Freddie had talked to two of them when he was buying his ticket. They were Communists[4] on their way to join the fight against the fascists in Spain. They seemed to know what they were doing. They told Freddie he didn't need a passport to get into France, but he would need one to cross into Spain. They told him where to get a train from Paris to Perpignan, near the border with Spain and a good place to cross the frontier without a passport. They even exchanged some French money for his English coins.

Freddie sat with his back against a lifeboat and took out his notebook. He opened it and smiled. The page was blank. The book was empty. *"Crossing to France, 14 August, 1936,"* he wrote. *"Nobody on this boat knows my face. Nobody in France knows my name. My life is starting again."*

Uncle Ruben and Aunt Isabel's farm, August 1936

Laura and Alonso watched the back door of the farmhouse. At about six, it opened and two dogs ran out, followed by their Aunt Isabel. Laura almost screamed out her aunt's name. They watched her feed the pigs and open up the henhouse. Aunt Isabel was their father's sister, and she looked just like him.

When the sun was overhead, Laura and Alonso decided to take a chance. They crept nearer to the house and crouched behind a woodpile. One of their cousins came out with the dogs, and Alonso shouted across the yard to him.

"Miguel! It's me, Alonso – your cousin. Can you call your dad?" Alonso and Laura stood up. Miguel turned and ran.

Alonso and Laura crouched down again. Their uncle came out, his gun at shoulder height, aiming toward the woodpile, the two dogs at his heels.

"Who's there?" he called.

"Uncle, it's me, Alonso," came a voice from behind the woodpile, "and Laura. We've escaped from Badajoz."

"Stand up slowly," said Uncle Ruben.

When he saw Laura and Alonso, he put his gun down and went toward them. Their aunt came running out of the house, followed by their cousins.

The family surrounded them, and everyone asked questions at once.

"Where's your father?" asked Uncle Ruben.

"We had to leave without him," said Alonso. "His leg was hurt when a bomb landed in the garden and he couldn't walk."

"Oh, poor Javier!" said Aunt Isabel.

"The rebels have probably taken him prisoner by now," said Laura.

"You'd better come inside," said their aunt. "If anyone sees you, we'll all be in trouble."

Their aunt and uncle agreed to let them stay. They had to keep out of sight as much as possible. And if anyone asked, they were their children – they all looked alike after all.

After dinner each night, Laura and Alonso climbed up a narrow staircase into the roof space, where their aunt had made them beds out of straw[5] and blankets. About a week after Laura and Alonso arrived, Uncle Ruben went into the nearest village for supplies. He came back with bad news. Badajoz had fallen to the Nationalists.

"What has happened to the people?" asked Laura. "Did you hear anything about Father?"

"The Nationalists have taken lots of prisoners," said Ruben, "but I couldn't find out anything about Javier."

That night, Laura couldn't sleep. Their aunt and uncle were in the room below. They spoke quietly, but not quietly enough. Laura had her ear to the floorboards.

"They can't stay here much longer," their uncle was saying. "It puts us all in danger. We'll be arrested – shot – we'll lose everything."

"They're my family – my little brother's children," protested their aunt. "Doesn't that mean anything?"

"There's no point in all of us dying," said their uncle. "Someone might see them . . . or one of the farm workers might tell the Nationalists. Who can you trust when we're all fighting each other?"

"So can they stay or can't they?" their aunt asked.

Laura held her breath. What would her uncle say? For a while, he didn't answer.

"They can stay here for now," whispered their uncle finally. "I won't turn them out."

Just then, there was a loud bang. Laura jumped. Alonso woke up.

"What's that?" cried her aunt in the room below.

Somebody was at the front door.

Chapter 3

What am I doing here?

France, August 1936

It was early morning in Paris, and shopkeepers were opening up. Freddie bought a long stick of bread. The day heated up as he wandered around the breathless city. He went inside the cool cavelike space of the great cathedral of Notre Dame, where he saw old men sleeping and two old ladies eating breakfast.

Toward lunchtime, Freddie climbed up a hill to the artists' quarter and looked down over the city. The atmosphere in Paris was electric, as if it was plugged in. He looked into artists' studios and saw a world that wasn't like his. Still in dressing gowns at midday, artists laughed and joked with their stylish models. One woman smiled at the innocent, open-mouthed country boy standing at the door. Freddie had never felt so alive.

By one o'clock, Freddie was starving. He found himself on a long avenue, where the wide pavements were filled with cafés. He chose a table almost out of sight and ordered a coffee. The tiny cup of strong black coffee arrived almost immediately. Nobody drank black coffee in Yorkshire. Freddie would have liked some milk with it, but he had no idea what the French for "milk" was.

He took out a postcard and started to write, as the sun bounced off the shiny round table. He'd chosen a picture of the Eiffel Tower.

"Dear Mum," he wrote, *"Don't worry – I'm in Paris and I'm safe. I'm on my way to Spain. Lots of foreign volunteers are going to the war, and I'm going with them. I'm sorry I didn't say good-bye properly, but I didn't want Dad to stop me. I want to have a go at being a journalist, and I hope one day Dad will be proud of me. Mum, you'll love Paris – I'll bring you here one day! Your son, Freddie"*

He didn't want to leave the café. He couldn't afford another coffee, so he hoped the waiter wouldn't notice him. The place had filled up now with clerks and shop assistants ordering lunch. Freddie tried not to look at the plates of food arriving on tables all around him.

"Can I sit here?" a man asked. He was wearing a black beret on his head and a striped sweater. Freddie smiled and made room for him. The man ordered lunch. Freddie glanced at him several times and wrote a description of him in his notebook. His face was generous, and his warm eyes were sharp and questioning. Once the man had finished his lunch, he took more interest in Freddie. He looked at the postcard lying on the table.

"Ah!" said the man in French. "You're English – you look German. Do you like Paris?"

"I'm afraid I don't speak French," Freddie said in English. The man looked at him blankly.

Freddie tried Spanish. *"Habla usted español?"*

"Yes, yes," replied the man in Spanish, with a wide smile. "I'm from Spain myself. So, do you like Paris?"

"Yes, sir," said Freddie. "It's very different from Yorkshire, where I come from!"

"And you are here . . . on holiday?"

"No," said Freddie, "I'm going to Spain. I'm a . . . I mean, I want to be a journalist. I want to write about the war."

The man called the waiter over and ordered more food and coffee.

"Are you a Communist?" he asked.

"No," said Freddie, "but I want the world to be a fairer place. People should be able to choose their own governments. Are you going back to fight?"

"I fight with my paintings – they are weapons. I don't paint pictures to put on the walls of houses," said the artist. "But I think perhaps I'm too old to fight with guns. I'm not a soldier. I only know about painting – I can't do anything else."

"Paintings – posters can be very powerful," said Freddie.

The waiter returned and placed an omelet and a piece of apple tart in front of Freddie.

"Oh, no," said Freddie. "I didn't order anything –"

The artist said something to the waiter.

"*Bon appétit*," the waiter said to Freddie and left them.

"I'm buying you lunch, young man," said the artist. "You can't go to war on an empty stomach."

While Freddie ate, the artist took out a pencil and a small book and started to draw.

"You're very young," said the artist when Freddie had finished. "Do you work for a newspaper?"

"I'm 18," lied Freddie. "I'm going to write for the *Yorkshire Evening Post.*"

"The world needs to know about this war," said the artist. "Britain, France – they must help the Spanish Republic."

The artist called the waiter over and paid the bill.

"And now I have work to do," he said.

"Thank you, sir," said Freddie.

"For you," said the artist, pulling a page from his sketchbook and handing it to Freddie.

"And in return, here is my description of you," said Freddie, tearing a page from his notebook and offering it to the artist.

"Thank you, young man," he said. "Please sign it. When you're a famous writer, I will remember this lunch."

At the post office, Freddie bought an envelope and sent the postcard and the drawing to his mother. Then he found the railway station and looked for trains going south. A train for Perpignan, near the Spanish border, was leaving in an hour or so. He hung around the station, watching other volunteers boarding. Just as the train was about to leave, he ran for it. A ticket inspector called to him, but Freddie carried on running, pointing to his bag.

"My ticket," he shouted in English, "it's at the bottom."

The train was moving now and he ran alongside, opened a carriage door, and jumped in. The carriage was nearly full, but he squeezed into a seat next to a young couple. The man had short dark hair and wore a gray suit. The woman wore a stylish hat and had red hair and a warm smile. Darkness began to fall over the French countryside and in the carriage. The rhythm of the train and the murmur of different languages soon sent Freddie to sleep.

Some hours later, Freddie woke and rubbed his neck. Daylight flooded through the windows and, further down the carriage, some men were singing. The couple next to him was talking quietly in a strange language.

Lines of trees and big open spaces went by, then thick forest. As the sun came up, it got hotter inside the train. The smell of unwashed bodies competed with the smell of garlic[6] sausage and cheese, as the travelers began to eat their breakfasts.

"Would you like something to eat?" asked the woman in the hat. She spoke in English and offered Freddie some bread and grapes.

"Thank you," said Freddie. She asked where he was from and where he was going. They were going to Barcelona, she said, to photograph the war. The man's name was Endre, and she was called Gerda.

"Where are you from?" Freddie asked.

"Endre is Hungarian," said Gerda. "And I'm German. We met in Paris."

"There's going to be fighting all over Europe – it's just starting in Spain," Gerda said. "There won't be any escape. Why are you going?"

"I'm kind of running away," said Freddie. "Life at home . . . well, it was like living in a cage."

"Ah, a young adventurer!" said Gerda, smiling.

"I want to fight, too," said Freddie.

Freddie chatted to Gerda and Endre for the rest of the journey.

"We're nearly there," said Endre, looking out of the window. "I can see Perpignan in the distance."

"I'll go and take a look," said Freddie.

He picked up his bag and walked through the carriage to the door. The last of the open countryside was flying by, and the border was up ahead.

"*Billets*," called the ticket inspector from the other end of the carriage. "Tickets, *billets*."

Freddie leaned out and saw the station in the distance. The inspector was halfway along the carriage now.

The train began to slow down. The inspector was checking Endre's ticket. Freddie's heart was beating fast. The signal up ahead was red, and the train was slowing right down now. A group of trees was coming up. As the train blew its whistle, Freddie leaned out of the window and opened the door from the outside. It swung open and he jumped.

"Hey!" shouted the inspector.

Freddie ran. He ran along a line of trees and then turned away from the train track into a field of lavender flowers. He heard the train's whistle again as it moved off into the town, and he slowed to a walk.

Twenty minutes later, he came to a stream running alongside a forest. He jumped across the little river, slipping on the banks in his Sunday shoes, and ran into the trees. The trees grew on a steep hill, and he ran up. He knew his journey into Spain crossed the Pyrenees mountains, so he had better get used to it. He ran on for some hours until he was exhausted and threw himself down on a bank. Sweat ran off his body as his heart calmed down and he fell asleep.

A branch broke near Freddie's head, and he woke. He sat up and looked around.

A small animal stared at him. What was it? It looked like a pig, but it had long hair and stripes. Freddie had never seen anything like it.

The wild boar piglet hesitated for a moment, then turned and ran.

"What am I doing here?" Freddie said aloud. He was starving and in a strange land. But he couldn't go back. Everyone in his hometown thought he had left the mine boss to die. It wasn't true, but he couldn't blame them for believing it. He had a reputation for being a coward, so they assumed that in a rock fall, Ralph would be brave and Freddie would try to run away. That all seemed a long way away now, sitting here on this wild hillside.

"Never mind the life story," he thought, "I need food."

He opened up a map he'd bought in Paris and located his position. A farm was marked about a kilometer ahead. It was early afternoon when he called to the farmer, who was leading a cow across his yard. Freddie did an afternoon's work for the farmer in exchange for food and a good night's sleep in the barn.

Setting off early the next morning, he headed for an isolated border town called Puigcerdà, where the Communists on the boat from England had told him it was easy to get into Spain. It took him two more days' walking before the border crossing came into view.

He waited until night fell, resting under an oak tree, and then got ready to cross into Spain.

"Ow," he moaned, as he pulled his shoes back onto his sore feet and thought of his comfortable work boots back at home. He checked his watch and packed up his bag.

But before he could get to his feet, he felt a gun at the back of his head.

LOOKING BACK

1 Check your answers to *Before you read* on page 4.

ACTIVITIES

2 <u>Underline</u> the correct words in each sentence about Chapter 1.

1 Freddie *can't bear / doesn't mind* going down into the mine.
2 Ralph *feels sorry for / laughs at* Freddie.
3 Freddie's *mother / father* is interested in world news.
4 Freddie and his dad have a *good / difficult* relationship.
5 Freddie is *popular / a bit of a loner*.
6 Freddie and Ralph fight over *the war in Spain / Freddie's sister*.
7 Ralph wants to *hurt Freddie / leave Freddie in peace*.

3 Put the sentences about Freddie in Chapters 1 and 3 in order.

1 An artist buys Freddie lunch in Paris. ☐
2 He pulls the boss free from the rocks. ☐
3 He crosses to France by boat. ☐
4 He decides to run away to Spain. ☐
5 He travels across France by train without a ticket. ☐
6 Mr. Taylor thanks Freddie before falling unconscious. ☐
7 Nobody from the town wants to talk to Freddie. ☐
8 Ralph takes the credit for saving the boss. ☐
9 The boss is trapped by falling rocks. ☐

4 Complete the sentences with the words in the box.

> the Republicans (x3)   the Nationalists (x3)

1 The rebel army fought for ....

2 .... supported the government.

3 Most of the Marcos family were in favor of ....

4 The fascists wanted .... to win the war.

5 Franco betrayed ....

6 .... didn't want a democratic government.

5 Answer the questions about Chapter 2.

1 A plane flies over Badajoz. What is it doing?

....

2 Why is Laura's father well known in the town?

....

3 Who is determined to fight for Spain – Laura or Alonso?

....

4 Why doesn't Uncle Ruben want Laura and Alonso to stay?

....

LOOKING FORWARD
• •

6 What do you think? Answer the questions.

1 Somebody bangs on the front door of the Sosa farm? Why?

....

2 Somebody holds something against Freddie's head? What?

....

Chapter 4

Prepare to fight!

Uncle Ruben's farm, late summer, 1936

Laura and Alonso kept still. The knocking continued at the front door. They heard their uncle run down the stairs.

"Who's there?" called Uncle Ruben.

A man with a strange accent answered. "Please, can you help me?" he called through the door. "I'm an American. I'm alone."

They heard Uncle Ruben and Aunt Isabel whispering.

"It may be a trap," hissed Uncle Ruben.

And then he spoke through the door to the man outside.

"Wait in the barn until daylight," said Uncle Ruben. "There's a tap in there – you can get fresh water."

"OK," called the voice. "And thank you."

Alonso looked down through a small window.

"He's walking across the yard to the barn," whispered Alonso.

"Can you see anyone else?" asked Laura.

"No, nothing's moving," said Alonso, yawning.

Laura still couldn't sleep and at first light, she heard the man come back toward the house. He stood in the middle of the yard.

The family watched from the house.

"I don't like it," said Uncle Ruben. "What's he doing here? How do we know he isn't going to shoot us?"

"Ruben," said Aunt Isabel. "You're a suspicious man. He looks sick to me – he needs our help. We mustn't let this war turn us into bad people."

"And you're far too trusting, Isabel," said Uncle Ruben. "He does look sick, though."

They watched for a few more minutes, but the man looked as if he was about to fall.

"OK," said Uncle Ruben. "We'll give him a chance."

Uncle Ruben and Alonso went out of the back door with guns to check for anyone hiding. They circled around to the front, aiming their rifles at the man. Laura and Aunt Isabel came out of the front door.

"I'm an American journalist," said the man in a weak voice. "The Nationalists are chasing me, and I'm trying to get back to Madrid, to the Republican zone."

"Why are they chasing you?" asked Uncle Ruben.

"I've come from Badajoz," he explained. "I saw terrible things there – a massacre. I wrote about it for my newspaper back in America. Now the Nationalists want to kill me."

"Go inside," said Uncle Ruben, pointing to the house with his gun. "Quickly."

"What did you see?" asked Laura in English, pushing in front of her aunt.

"Be patient, Laura," said Aunt Isabel. "Let him come in and sit down. We'll hear the news later."

The American came inside. His clothes were damp, his body was shaking, and his forehead was wet with sweat.

"He's got a temperature," said Aunt Isabel, heating up some soup for him.

"When can we ask him?" whispered Laura to her aunt.

"The man's sick," said Aunt Isabel. "He must rest. No questions, OK?"

"OK," said Laura.

After a good sleep, the American was able to talk for a while.

"Before you start," said Uncle Ruben, "you're leaving as soon as the fever's gone. Don't tell us your name. The less we know, the better."

"Sure," said the American. "I'll tell you what I know."

He spoke in English, and Laura and Alonso translated. "I went into Badajoz a week ago. The fighting was over, and the

Nationalists were in control of the city. Many lives had already been lost in the street fighting on both sides. I interviewed Colonel Yagüe – the Nationalist leader. He said he wanted to teach the Republicans a lesson, so his men killed – murdered – all the Republican soldiers they found."

"What happened to the townspeople?" asked Laura.

"Yagüe's men rounded up any Republican supporters – they dragged people out of their houses. There were no trials – there was no kind of justice. One man could say about his neighbor, "He's a Red. He's always hated the Catholic[7] Church," and no questions were asked – the neighbor was dragged off. So they rounded up thousands of people – I don't know exactly how many. They marched them all down to the bullring and shot them. Every one of them. It was a massacre."

The American closed his eyes.

"You're exhausted," said Aunt Isabel. "You mustn't talk anymore."

Laura ran out of the house to the barn. Alonso followed and tried to comfort his sister, but it was hard. He shared her despair.

"Do you think Father's dead?" said Laura, tears running down her cheeks.

"No, I refuse to believe it," said Alonso. "He must have gotten away somehow."

"Why is this evil happening?" cried Laura.

"I don't know," said Alonso. "But you were right. This is our war, and we must fight it."

Over the next two days, the American recovered. Laura looked after him, first nursing him and then keeping him company. She asked him hundreds of questions about life in America, and he told her all about Chicago. He told her about the jazz clubs and his favorite baseball team, the Chicago White Sox.

"Chicago!" she said, enjoying the word. "It sounds so romantic . . . so free. One day I will visit Chicago."

On the third day, Uncle Ruben asked the American to leave.

He thanked the Sosa family for their hospitality. "And thank you, Laura, for bringing me back to life," he said. "Don't forget to look me up when you get to Chicago."

"I don't even know your name," she laughed.

The French border, on the same day

"Hands up!" said a voice in Spanish.

Freddie slowly put his hands up.

"I'm English," said Freddie, his voice shaking.

"Why didn't you say so?"

Freddie turned around. A tall, strong-looking man was holding a piece of metal pipe.

"That's not much of a gun," said Freddie.

"I didn't say I had a gun," said the man. "Which side are you on?" asked the man.

"Republican," said Freddie.

"Correct answer. I'm Ray," said the man, holding out his hand.

"You're American," said Freddie.

"Yup. I'm planning to cross the border tonight," said Ray. "But why are you creeping around?"

"No papers," said Freddie. "I haven't got a passport. My name's Freddie, by the way. You seem to be creeping about, too."

"I've got a passport, but I didn't have a train ticket, so I jumped off the train outside Perpignan. A French farmer was driving up here – he offered to take me."

"Lucky you!" said Freddie. "I jumped off, too, but walked all the way up here. Are you heading to Barcelona?"

"Yeah," said Ray.

"Maybe we could travel together?"

"Let's get over the border first. I heard that the Anarchists[8] control the border checkpoint[9] here," said Ray. "They're on the Republican side, and they won't care about passports as long as we're Republicans, too."

39

"'Are you sure?" said Freddie.

"If they turn us back," said Ray, "we'll just walk along the border a little way and go straight over. There aren't many border patrols. One thing though."

"What's that?" asked Freddie.

"Don't look so worried," laughed Ray.

Ray was right. The border guards waved them through.

"Bring guns next time," they said in Spanish. "But thank you for coming to fight for freedom. Good luck!"

Uncle Ruben's farm, later the same day

It was just getting dark when Aunt Isabel put dinner on the table.

"Laura," she said. "Call Alonso and Miguel – they're still out in the barn." But suddenly Miguel appeared at the door with Alonso right behind him.

"Two motorbikes," shouted Miguel, "and an army truck – coming up the track."

"Come on, Laura," said Alonso, already halfway up to the roof space. Aunt Isabel removed their places from the table.

"Ruben Sosa," said an army captain, marching into the house with two soldiers behind him. Uncle Ruben turned around to face him.

"Yes," said Uncle Ruben.

"There's a rumor in Mérida that you're hiding some Republicans," said the captain. "I'm sure the information is unreliable. I know you would never be so foolish."

There was a pause.

"Of course it isn't true, er, Lieutenant," said Aunt Isabel quickly, guessing at his rank.

"Captain," the man corrected her.

"People will say anything these days," said Aunt Isabel.

"And, Señor Sosa, are you a supporter of General Franco?" asked the captain.

"My nephew, Esteban Marcos, is a major in General Franco's army. We're very proud of Esteban," said Uncle Ruben.

"I'm glad to hear it," said the captain. "Now we have an army to feed, Señor Sosa. We need whatever you have on the farm – meat, grain, vegetables. I'm going to leave these two men on the farm. Please provide them with food and beds."

"We will be pleased to serve the army, Captain," said Uncle Ruben.

"Good," said the captain. "That will be all. Long live Spain!"

The two soldiers stood at the door.

"Welcome, gentlemen," said Aunt Isabel. "Please take your boots off and sit at the table. My husband will get your room ready while I serve you supper. Wine?"

Laura and Alonso heard their uncle and Miguel rearranging furniture in the children's bedroom. Aunt Isabel looked after the two soldiers, filling their wine glasses several times. Although it was August, it was quite cold in the evening, and Uncle Ruben built up the kitchen fire, making the room hotter and hotter. Laura and her brother silently changed their clothes. Their bags were already packed. They waited and listened.

Sometime later, the soldiers' heads hit the table as they finally fell asleep. Uncle Ruben came upstairs quietly to the roof space. He signaled to his nephew and niece to come down. Alonso came down first, tiptoeing past the sleeping soldiers. He waited outside the front door in the shadows. Uncle Ruben went back up the stairs to get Laura.

"Where are you going?" shouted one of the men, aiming his rifle up the main stairs. "What's up there?"

"It's just me," Uncle Ruben shouted back.

"He's going to get some bedclothes," said Aunt Isabel. "We're making up beds for the children in our room – so you can sleep in their room."

"Hmph," said the soldier. He sat up and watched Uncle Ruben bring blankets down and take them into the bedroom. Then Uncle Ruben closed the door into the roof space and showed the men their room.

"You get some sleep," said the man with the rifle to the other soldier. "I'll stay in the kitchen tonight."

"Fine," said Uncle Ruben. "You'll be more comfortable upstairs, though."

"I'll decide where I'm comfortable," said the soldier.

The family went to bed, and the soldier stayed on watch.

At dawn, Laura crept down the ladder from the roof space and then down the main stairs into the kitchen and went to the front door, silently putting her hand on the handle. One of the dogs growled.

"Who's there?" said the soldier, waking up at once. Laura opened the door wide, and he blinked as the bright sunlight blinded him.

"It's just me – Señora de Sosa," she said, not looking at him. "I'm going out to open the henhouse and feed the pigs."

The soldier said nothing but seemed to go back to sleep. A few moments later, Alonso peered out from behind a pile of straw. "Aunt Isabel," he whispered. "Where's Laura?"

"It's me," said Laura, taking off Aunt Isabel's dress.

Just then, Uncle Ruben appeared in the barn door. He gave them a bag of food from the kitchen.

"I'm so sorry," he said to his niece and nephew. "It's too dangerous to stay here with us. I went to school with that captain who brought the men here, and he knows how many children I have."

Laura and Alonso hugged their uncle.

"Take care," said Uncle Ruben. "I hope we will meet again in happier times."

They headed east, avoiding other farms and villages and following the River Guadiana where they could. They had to cross several streams and wider sections of water. The land climbed up into some hills, and they found a small cave to hide in during daylight.

Laura untied her long dark hair, and it fell around her shoulders. She searched around in her backpack and pulled out a pair of scissors.

"Here," she said, handing the scissors to Alonso. "If I'm going to save the Republic, I need to look the part!"

Alonso cut through the thick hair and handed it to Laura.

"You're too pretty to be a boy," he said.

"I don't want to look like a boy," said Laura. "I want to be a woman of the Republic – strong and equal to you men. No more long hair and skirts for me!"

She laid her hair on a rock.

"I'll leave this here," she said. "The birds can use it for their nests next spring . . . if spring ever comes again."

She wore Miguel's clothes, which fitted well, with a cap over her new haircut.

"Of course, I realize that you're my equal," said Alonso. "But if we run into trouble with any Nationalists, keep your head down and let me talk. We'll say you're my younger brother."

"Why are we suddenly foreigners in our own country?" she said. "Hiding in caves and wearing disguises."

"We'll be safe when we get to Madrid. There's no way the rebels can take the capital," he said. "They'd need more help from outside."

It took them several nights' walking to get near to Ciudad Real. They decided to try and take a train north to Toledo and then on to Madrid.

They realized they were in the Republican zone when they saw trucks with government flags on the road, and they felt safe enough to travel by day. Just outside Ciudad Real, they stopped for a rest, sitting in the shade of an old olive tree.

Suddenly Laura screamed and jumped up.

"What's up?" asked Alonso.

"Look at the ground!" she said. "It's blood. And it isn't very old."

"And look at this," said Alonso. "Empty bullet cases. There's been some shooting here."

"We're in Republican territory now," said Laura. "I wonder what happened."

"Maybe some local people sympathized with the Nationalists," said Alonso. "And . . ."

Laura began to cry. "I keep thinking of father in that bullring," she said.

Alonso put his arms around her. "We don't know he was even there," he said. "We mustn't think that. He had a letter from Esteban, remember? Like the one we've got. Maybe that saved him."

"I hate this war," shouted Laura.

They came down a hill into Ciudad Real about an hour later. Shops and banks were opening after siesta, and people were going to work. Laura and Alonso bought newspapers and took them to a café. The news was shocking.

"*'Franco's rebels poised to attack Madrid,'*" Laura read aloud, "Oh no!"

"I didn't think he'd get there so fast," said Alonso.

Just then, the café owner turned up the radio. It was a woman's voice.

"Young men of the Republic, prepare to fight! Young women of the Republic, prepare to fight! We must defend our freedom against the fascist Franco and the Nationalist army! We must defend Madrid against the Nationalists! Long live the Republic! The Nationalists must not pass! They will not pass! *No pasarán!*"

Everyone in the café stood up.

"*No pasarán!*" they shouted and held their fists in the air.

Chapter 5

Show me your papers

Northern Spain, September 1936

At first light, Freddie and Ray got a lift on a truck heading from the French border to Berga, about 40 kilometers into Spain, to pick up some rifles. The truck climbed slowly up the mountain road and then raced down the other side. They'd been up all night, but there was no chance of sleeping on this ride. They were glad they hadn't had any breakfast. In Berga, the driver took them to a restaurant and introduced them to the owner.

"Foreign volunteers," he explained.

The owner gave them a free breakfast. The driver showed them a room at the back of the restaurant, where they could get some sleep.

"Hey!" said Ray when he woke up some hours later. "Where's my watch?"

"I bet the driver stole it," said Freddie, rubbing his eyes. "I saw him looking at it while we were eating breakfast."

They were high up in the mountains, and the air was delicious, but it was getting colder as the light faded. They set off down the main road toward Barcelona.

"I know you hate the fascists and all that, but why are you here?" said Freddie. "Why are you even in Europe?"

"I got into a little trouble back home," said Ray. "I thought I'd better leave town for a while."

Freddie waited for Ray to continue.

"I was working on a building site in Manhattan – on a skyscraper," said Ray. "But then the money ran out, and they stopped building. I couldn't get any work after that. There aren't any jobs in the United States right now. So, anyway, I ended up living in tent city – Hooverville, they call it, in Central Park in New York. Life is pretty tough there."

"That's bad luck, Ray," said Freddie.

"Yeah, and you can't live on nothing in New York. So, you know, I had to help myself to stay alive. I stole some tools from the building site, and one of the guards saw me. I had to disappear after that, so I worked my way to Europe on a cruise ship."

The road climbed steeply, and they didn't talk for a while.

"New York!" said Freddie, as they reached the top of a hill and looked down on a dramatic green valley. "Wow! I love that bit in *King Kong* where he climbs to the top of the Empire State Building – I can't believe you worked on a skyscraper. What's it like at the top?"

"Well, you sure get a good view."

"We don't have any skyscrapers in Yorkshire," said Freddie. "The jobs in my town are under the ground."

"What – mining?" asked Ray.

"Yeah, coal mining," explained Freddie. "How come your Spanish is so good?"

"I worked with a South American crew[10] on the construction site," said Ray. "I guess I just picked it up. How about you? Your Spanish isn't bad."

"My mum and I have been teaching ourselves," he said. "Every first of January she starts learning something new. This year it was Spanish."

Toward dusk, they came around a bend in the road to a crossroad. The signpost pointing left showed the town of Manresa was 30 kilometers away, so they found somewhere off the road to sleep.

When they woke the next morning, their clothes were wet through from the grass, but as soon as the sun came up, they started to dry off. They spent another day marching along the dusty road. Ray entertained Freddie with stories of his love life.

He was handsome and easy-going, and it seemed that many women fell for his charm. Finally Manresa came into view in the distance. The lights of the railway station sparkled against the darkening sky.

A train was waiting at the station platform. There were armed guards all along the platform and on the train, holding automatic rifles. Freddie and Ray tried to go into the station, but a soldier came toward them and pushed them back.

"What's going on?" asked Ray.

"Government business," said the soldier. He had a long, thin scar down his cheek. "The railway station is closed. Come back tomorrow."

"Where's the train going?" asked Ray. Freddie was already walking away.

The soldier replied by aiming his gun at Ray.

"OK, OK," said Ray, holding up his hands and backing off.

"There must be someone important on that train," said Freddie.

"Or some *thing*," said Ray.

Ray and Freddie went on toward the center of town, crossing the tracks by a footbridge and keeping an eye on the soldier with the scar, who was keeping an eye on them. Then the soldier disappeared inside the station building.

"Come on," said Ray to Freddie, grabbing his arm urgently. "This way."

They ran north, parallel with the track, hidden from the soldiers on the station platform by a freight[11] train. Around a corner, they slid down the bank to the tracks.

"Let's take a free ride," said Ray. "We can be in Barcelona before the restaurants close."

"There are soldiers all over the train," said Freddie. "We'll get shot!"

The train appeared around the corner, and Ray and Freddie watched it move slowly past them. Then it came to a stop right next to them. It was taking on coal. Ray and Freddie looked at each other. All they had to do was climb onto the step on the back of the last car.

Ten minutes later, the train was speeding through the night. Freddie looked through a small window into the car. A few soldiers were playing cards, their rifles leaning against large boxes around them. Some men in suits, who didn't look very Spanish, sat separately.

Ray and Freddie spent the whole trip outside on the little step. Although it was August, the rushing air froze their fingers and toes. The train stopped outside Barcelona station, and the soldiers began to get off the front half of the train. It was completely dark, but Ray and Freddie could hear their voices. Some of them were walking along the side of the train to the back. They banged on the car windows and shouted to the soldiers inside, laughing and joking.

"Come on," Ray whispered to Freddie, jumping off the back of the train onto the track. "Let's get out of here."

Their voices were coming nearer.

"Freddie!" hissed Ray, and he disappeared around the side of the train.

But Freddie wasn't moving. As a feeling of panic rose through his body, he tried to breathe deeply. By the time he had control of his arms and legs, the first soldier had almost reached the back of the train. Any second now, he would see Freddie standing on the little platform.

But just before the soldier appeared, the car door next to Freddie opened from the inside, hiding him from view.

"Hurry up!" shouted someone from inside the car.

"We're coming – keep your shirt on," said the first soldier.

The soldiers jumped onto the platform one by one and went into the car. The last one pulled the car door shut behind him.

The train began to move again, very slowly, into the station. A hand grabbed Freddie's arm and pulled him down onto the tracks.

Freddie followed Ray across several sets of tracks to a fence. They followed the fence until it joined the end of a platform.

"Do what I do," Ray hissed to Freddie.

The two men walked casually along the platform. There was a bar next to the exit. Ray ordered two coffees and paid with a few peseta coins he had in his pocket. He drank his coffee in one mouthful.

"OK, Freddie, what was that all about?" Ray asked in a low, tense voice. "You nearly got us killed."

"I'm sorry, Ray," said Freddie. "I just freeze sometimes. When I get in a difficult situation . . ."

"That was so close," said Ray.

"I get this feeling of panic," Freddie went on. "When I got stuck in the elevator in the mine, I just, you know, couldn't handle it."

"You'd better learn to handle it, Freddie," said Ray, "or you won't be any use to anyone. This is a war, Freddie. It's not the school playground."

"I'm learning to control it, Ray," said Freddie. "There was an accident in the mine just before I left. Part of the tunnel roof came down, and my boss was caught. Yes, I was frightened at first. You would have been, too. But then I pulled him out and saved him from a second fall."

"Hmm," said Ray.

"Don't you believe me?" asked Freddie.

"How do I know?" said Ray. "I wasn't there."

"Give me a break, Ray," said Freddie. "I'm not a coward."

"I didn't say you were a coward, Freddie," said Ray, pushing Freddie's coffee along the bar to him.

Just then, some soldiers came to the bar – the ones from the train. And there was the soldier with the scar from the station in Manresa – the one who had waved his gun at them. Freddie turned his back and signaled to Ray with his eyes. Ray turned away, too. They moved further down the bar where it was darker.

The Spanish soldiers were talking loudly and laughing. The other men from the train were speaking a different language.

"I don't understand what they're saying," said Freddie, "but I think they're speaking Russian."

"Russians! We're lucky they didn't catch us," said Ray. "They wouldn't ask questions; they'd just shoot us."

"The Russians must be helping the Republic," said Freddie. "And what's in those boxes on that train? Weapons, maybe?"

"I don't think we'll ask them," said Ray.

"Hey!" said a voice behind them in Spanish. "Weren't you at the station in Manresa? How did you get here so fast?"

Ray and Freddie turned around. It was the soldier with the scar.

"There was another train right after yours – a fast train," said Ray.

"Show me your papers," said the soldier suspiciously.

Ray reached into his pocket for his passport. The soldier checked it.

"American?" he said. He sounded impressed. "Why are you here?"

"To fight for the Republic," said Ray.

The soldier turned to Freddie. "And you?" he said, holding out his hand. "Papers."

The soldier looked at Freddie. Ray looked at Freddie.

Freddie looked at the soldier's long, thin scar. It burned red in the electric light. Freddie had no papers.

Chapter 6

Is it worth dying for?

Barcelona, September 1936

"Papers!" repeated the soldier in Spanish.

"I'm sorry," said Ray. "He's English. He doesn't speak Spanish. Let me explain. His passport was stolen. A truck driver gave us a ride to Berga. He took my watch and Freddie's passport while we were asleep."

"Follow me," said the soldier.

"Me, too?" asked Ray.

"No, you can go. Just this boy," said the soldier.

Ray squeezed Freddie's arm. "Meet me at the main post office," he whispered. "Just act stupid – pretend you don't understand anything. You're a foreigner – they won't hurt you. Good luck."

Freddie followed the soldier into the stationmaster's office. Another soldier came in.

"Who's this?" he asked.

"Just some stupid foreign boy," said the soldier with the scar.

"Can we check these details about the boxes?" said the second soldier, looking at Freddie.

"Don't worry," said the soldier with the scar. "You can talk. The boy doesn't understand Spanish."

They had a long conversation about some gold in the boxes on the train. Freddie understood every word. It was government gold, going to Moscow to pay for Russian weapons and planes. Then they discussed Freddie.

"Is he a spy? He doesn't look dangerous," said the second soldier.

"His friend said they were here to fight for the Republic," said the soldier with the scar.

"I'll call the Russians," said the second soldier.

"No," said the soldier with the scar. "He's our prisoner – we can decide what to do with him."

But then the Russians came in, and the two soldiers explained why Freddie was there.

The Russians said a few words to each other in Russian and then turned to go. At the door, the last Russian turned and said two words in Spanish to the soldier with the scar.

"Shoot him," he said.

The soldiers looked at each other, and they looked at Freddie.

"OK," said the soldier with the scar. "I'll do it."

He marched Freddie out onto the platform and out of the station. He took him around the side of the main building, into a dark alley. He lifted his rifle.

Freddie closed his eyes and waited for the shot.

The shot didn't come. Instead the soldier spoke.

"Go!" he said.

"Go?" repeated Freddie.

"Go!" hissed the soldier again, pushing Freddie along the alley.

He raised his rifle and shot into the air. The sound nearly deafened Freddie.

"Run away. This is Spain. We're not ruled by Moscow yet, and I don't take orders from Russians."

Freddie didn't wait to hear more. He disappeared into the shadowy streets of Barcelona, grateful to be alive.

After asking a few people for directions, a friendly old man led him to the international press office.

Freddie explained that he had an important story and was taken to see a British journalist named Frank. Freddie told Frank about the gold on the train and reported the conversations he had overheard in the stationmaster's office. Frank was impressed.

"You've got a good eye for details," Frank told him. "And a good ear for a story. You could be a good journalist one day." And he offered him a job.

"As a journalist?" Freddie asked.

"Er . . . not exactly," Frank said. "We're looking for an office boy – someone to make the coffee and telegraph our stories. You'll probably have to buy us illegal soap and sausages, too. We might give you a press card, though."

Freddie thought for a moment and then spoke. "I'm here with an American friend, and we're going to the front to fight."

"Fine," Frank said. "Good luck with that. And thanks for the story." He swung his chair back to his typewriter and went back to work.

Later Freddie found the main post office. When Ray came whistling up the road that afternoon, they greeted each other like old friends.

"I was worried," Ray said, after Freddie told him the story. "Those Russians looked dangerous."

"So where do we go to join up?" Freddie wondered.

"There doesn't seem to be one Republican army," said Ray. "I've been stopping people in uniform and asking them who they're fighting with. There are different groups – Communists, Anarchists, Socialists[12] – I'm confused."

They spent the next few weeks in the city, deciding what to do. More foreign volunteers were arriving every day, and there was talk of setting up international brigades for them. They were going to be based several hundred kilometers further south. Ray and Freddie decided to go there.

They packed up their things and went to the railway station. Ray looked at Freddie as they lined up to buy tickets.

"I've been thinking, Freddie," said Ray. "I don't think you should come – not yet anyway."

"What do you mean?" protested Freddie.

"Freddie, if I had to attack fascist troops, I wouldn't want you next to me," he said. "I like you, Freddie, but, honestly, you're not brave enough for war – or maybe not old enough. Remember what happened on the gold train?"

"I've never even held a gun in my life," Freddie started to defend himself. "When I've had some training –"

"Training won't help you. It's in your mind. There's plenty you can do here. You can help in a hospital, drive an ambulance, or take that job at the press office," said Ray.

"Do I have a choice?" said Freddie.

"Don't look so miserable," said Ray. "Go on, admit it. You don't want to fight, do you?"

"I want to be part of this," said Freddie. "But maybe you're right. Maybe I'm just a coward."

"I'm not saying you're a coward – you're just not ready," said Ray. "I predict that one day you'll be a hero," he joked.

They shook hands, and Freddie left the line and the station. He'd only been in Spain a few weeks and there was that word again – coward. It followed him everywhere. He breathed in deeply. Then he went straight back to the press office and asked for Frank.

Madrid, September 1936

"Ow!" cried Laura, as she dropped a stone on her foot. She and Alonso were in the Plaza de Atocha in the center of the city, helping to build barricades[13]. People on one side of the square were digging up the streets. Lines of old men, women, and children were passing the stones to the other side. When the soldiers told everyone to stop for the day, they put their arms above their heads to stretch their backs.

Laura and her brother walked around the square to inspect the barricades. There were posters and flags pinned up. "*Victory to the Republic!*" they said and "*Freedom from fascism!*"

Laura stopped suddenly, her hand over her mouth.

"What's wrong?" said Alonso.

She pointed to one of the flags. It said, "*In Badajoz, the fascists shot 4,000. If Madrid falls, they will shoot half the city.*"

"The fascists are destroying our country, Laura," said Alonso. "I would give my life to stop them."

"You've changed, Alonso," said Laura. "You wouldn't have said that back in Badajoz."

"No, you were always the political one," he said. "But in the last two months, I've grown up. We must fight to keep the Republic."

They returned to their room in a small hotel in Plaza de Santa Ana, next to the Spanish Theater. The room was like a matchbox and not very clean, but it was cheap.

Nationalist tanks and soldiers were pointing their guns at the city from the east and the southwest. Madrid was filling with more and more refugees every day, and Laura and her brother were lucky to have a room at all. That evening, they went across to their local café for supper. They found a table in a corner and ordered.

A group of soldiers came in just after them and sat at the next table. One of the men glanced toward them several times during the meal. Laura began to feel uncomfortable, and they got up to leave.

"We need more men," said one of the soldiers to Alonso. "When are you joining up?"

"We're working every day on the barricades," said Alonso. "I'll be fighting, don't you worry. But I'm looking after my sister."

"Oh," said Laura. "I'll join up, too."

"We're not taking women soldiers in our unit," said the soldier.

"Unless she's a good cook," laughed another soldier. "Our food is disgusting."

They all laughed, and Alonso came toward them with his fist raised.

"Calm down," said the first soldier. "Apologies for my colleague, *señorita*."

Laura and Alonso left the café. It was dark now, and the streets were empty. They saw a patrol entering the little square, and they ran across to their hotel.

*   *   *

A long line of trucks pulled out of Madrid, taking the government to Valencia. The citizens of Madrid were terrified and felt abandoned, but some of the soldiers preferred no government.

"Long live Madrid without a government!" they shouted.

The next morning, Laura and Alonso couldn't cross the Paseo del Prado. There were thousands of sheep in the way. The rebels had pushed farmers off their lands, and the farmers were driving their sheep through the center of the city to the west side.

"This war gets stranger by the minute," said Alonso. "Who's that artist you like?"

"Salvador Dalí?"

"He'd like this," Alonso smiled.

Just then, they heard the planes of the Nationalist air force on their way. People crowded down into the subway stations. The sheep had to look after themselves. There were small explosions all over the city. Then the Republican planes came in from the west and attacked the Nationalist planes. People came back out onto the streets to watch. When a plane was hit, they shouted and cheered, hoping it was one of Franco's planes.

After the battle in the air, daily life continued as normal. The butchers, the banks, and the tailors opened, even though they didn't have many customers or much to sell. Alonso went to dig trenches. Laura went to the Ritz Hotel. There were no rich guests checking in at the hotel anymore, only refugees from the countryside. Today she was sent to the ballroom to help with handing out clothes and blankets. When the planes came back over, the great chandeliers rocked above their heads.

That evening, Alonso rushed into their little room. Laura was sitting in front of the mirror, trying to cut her hair straighter.

"I'm so bad at this," she said.

"Listen to this!" he said, catching his breath. "I was digging trenches with some soldiers this afternoon. Then they were going out on a patrol and asked me to go with them. So we went along behind our front line. And there was a place where a Nationalist tank had broken through our lines – one of Franco's tanks – but then it had been knocked out by an anti-tank attack from our side. We opened up the tank –"

"Was there anyone still inside?" asked Laura.

"Yeah, get this . . . we opened up and pulled out three fascists, including a captain."

"Was he dead?"

Alonso nodded. "They all were. The soldiers laid the bodies out on the ground. They took their watches, guns, and all that and then looked inside the tank. So I started going through their inside pockets, and I found some documents."

"What were they?" asked Laura.

"They were plans for the attack on Madrid! Starting tomorrow! So we all jumped back into the truck and drove as fast as we could to Republican headquarters and handed them over."

"Alonso!" said Laura, giving her brother a hug. "You've just saved Madrid!"

Laura looked at her brother. His eyes were on fire.

"You know, Laura," he said, "when I think what they have done to us – to our family, to our futures . . . they mustn't win."

"Finally you see it the way I do," said Laura. "But what about Esteban? He's part of it."

"He's no brother of mine," said Alonso.

The skies were darkening outside.

"I'm hungry," said Laura. "Let's go and eat."

"You go over to the café," said her brother. "I'll be over in a minute. I want to clean up a bit first."

Laura sat at their usual table. She picked up a paper. "*General Franco will soon be drinking coffee in Madrid's main square*," it said.

She threw the paper down.

Alonso came into the café. He had a bag behind his back and hid it under his chair before Laura noticed it.

"What would you like?" asked Laura.

"I'm not hungry," he said, "I don't want anything."

"Are you OK?" asked Laura.

"I'm fine," he said. "Maybe I'll have a cold drink."

Laura ordered a drink for Alonso and bean stew[14] for herself. Alonso kept glancing around the café. He seemed to find it hard to look at Laura.

"Something's wrong. What is it?" she asked.

"I've got something to tell you," he said. "I've signed up. I'm collecting my uniform this evening."

"What do you mean?" cried Laura.

"I've joined the army," he said.

"Where are you going?" said Laura.

"North of the city," he said. "Toward Guadalajara. We're moving up there tomorrow."

"And . . . what about me?"

"I've bought you a ticket for Barcelona. You'll be safe there."

"How long have you been planning this?" asked Laura quietly.

"I wasn't ready to fight before," said Alonso. "I was too scared. But now it's win or die for me."

"Can I join, too?" asked Laura.

"You know that's impossible, Laura," said Alonso. "But there'll be war work in Barcelona. And you'll be safer there."

They paid and left the café. Outside in the street, Alonso put his arms around his sister.

"Is this it?" she asked.

"This is it," he said. "You'll be all right, won't you?"

"Yes, of course," she said.

"Keep checking the post office in Barcelona," he said. "We can write to each other there."

"What if the fascists win?" said Laura.

"Then we'll meet up in Barcelona," said Alonso. "And if that falls, try and get to Saint Jean de Luz in France. Mother's brother is there – he'll help you. We can find each other there."

". . . if you're still alive," said Laura. "Is it worth dying for?"

"Are you really saying that to me?" asked Alonso, surprised. "You're the one who's made me believe in all this."

"Me and General Franco," said Laura. "It's just . . . when it comes to saying good-bye, it's not so easy."

"I have to do this – I have to fight," he said. "And I know you feel the same."

He kissed his sister and left her.

"What about your things?" she called after him.

He held up the bag he was carrying, but he didn't look back.

At the hotel, Laura sat on her bed. Alonso had left the letter from Esteban, the rest of their money, and the ticket to Barcelona in a neat pile.

She had never felt so alone.

The Times

REPUBLICANS TRIUMPH IN MADRID!
FASCISTS FAIL TO TAKE CAPITAL

GENERAL FRANCO TO CONTINUE FIGHT:
"I'll destroy Madrid rather than leave it to the Reds"

LOOKING BACK

● ●

1 Check your answers to *Looking forward* on page 35.

ACTIVITIES

● ●

2 Match the two parts of the sentences about Chapter 4.

1 The Nationalists want to kill the American ☐
2 Freddie and Ray have both come to Spain ☐
3 The border guards wave them into Spain ☐
4 Laura gets out of the house ☐
5 Laura cuts her hair short ☐
6 In Ciudad Real, Laura and Alonso learn that ☐

a by disguising herself as her aunt.
b because they didn't like his newspaper reports.
c the army has nearly entered Madrid.
d to fight for the Republic.
e to show that women are equal to men in the Republic.
f without asking for their passports.

3 Read the sentences and write *F* (Freddie), *R* (Ray), *B* (both) or *?* (the answer isn't in the text).

1 He has come to Spain because of trouble at home. ☐
2 His watch is stolen. ☐
3 He speaks Spanish. ☐
4 Women often fall in love with him. ☐
5 He doesn't want to get on the train. ☐
6 He asks the soldier with the scar about the boxes on the train. ☐
7 He shows the soldier his passport. ☐

4 Are the sentences about Chapter 6 true (*T*) or false (*F*)?

1 Freddie can't understand what the soldiers are saying. ☐
2 The soldier with the scar doesn't like the Russians. ☐
3 Frank offers Freddie a job as a journalist. ☐
4 Ray thinks Freddie is ready to be a great soldier. ☐
5 Freddie decides to take Frank's offer of a job. ☐
6 In Madrid, Laura helps at a refugee center. ☐
7 Alonso finds Nationalist plans for a new tank. ☐
8 Alonso discusses his plans with Laura before he joins the army. ☐

5 Complete the sentences with the adjectives in the box.

alone	thankful	bitter	proud	scared

1 The American journalist is .... to the Sosa family for their hospitality. (page 39)

2 Laura and Alonso feel .... when they shout "*No pasarán!*" in the café. (page 45)

3 Freddie is .... when the soldiers are approaching the back of the train. (page 50)

4 Freddie feels .... when Ray tells him he's not ready to fight. (page 56)

5 Laura feels very .... when Alonso leaves her in Madrid. (page 63)

LOOKING FORWARD
• •

6 What do you think? Answer the question.

Who do you think says "Welcome to Barcelona"?

....

Chapter 7

Welcome to Barcelona

Barcelona, May 1937

"This will cost you two packs of American cigarettes," said the man, pulling a can of sardines[15] out of a deep pocket.

Freddie held out a second pack. The man gave him the can and ran off down the Ramblas, a wide, tree-lined street.

"That wasn't exactly a bargain," thought Freddie. Some of the American journalists gave out cigarettes at the press office. Freddie didn't smoke, but they were useful currency. For buying sardines, for example.

Freddie hid the can deep inside his jacket. He reached his building and climbed up the stairs to the top floor, to his room overlooking a tiny square.

Freddie had been in Barcelona for nearly a year. It was May, and the cold winter had given way to a gray spring. As he enjoyed his sardines, he thought back to his last conversation with Ray. If he had insisted on going with Ray, he would probably be lying dead on a battlefield now. Instead, he was part of the press team, learning to be a writer, mixing with top journalists. OK, so he hadn't actually sent off any articles yet, but he was right at the heart of things now.

In the evening, Freddie left his room and walked to the press office. He spent a couple of hours listening to English language radio stations, writing down anything interesting. He checked incoming telegraphs at the same time, and that evening the machines were busy.

Frank sat at his desk in the corner of the same room.

"Ever heard of a place called Guernica, Frank?" called Freddie.

"Yeah," he said, his fingers tapping on a typewriter. "It's in the Basque country, up in the north of Spain. Has the rebel army captured it?"

"Something's going on there," said Freddie. "One report says that the town is being flattened by bombs dropped from German planes."

Frank nodded and continued typing.

Freddie went into the Spanish press office. In the middle of the noise of typewriters, telephones, and telegraph machines, he discovered more about Guernica. Different stories were coming in. *"Basque Reds set fire to their own city,"* said one. *"Nationalists bomb town by mistake,"* said another. *"Germans and Italians destroy Basque town,"* said a third.

Over the next few days, more information arrived. There were still many different stories, but more and more accounts agreed on what had happened that day: German and Italian planes had bombed the town for several hours continuously. Fighter planes had flown low over the town and machine-gunned people running from the bombs. Some journalists were there. As he read their eyewitness accounts one afternoon, Freddie could feel their shock. "*I have seen many wars in many lands,*" wrote one French journalist, "*but I have never seen horror like this.*"

Later, Frank gave him a pack of letters.

"Take these to the post office, Freddie," he said. "They need to go tonight."

BARCELONA: COMMUNISTS AND ANARCHISTS IN STREET FIGHTS

Freddie ran down the road to the big post office. He went into the building and joined the shortest line. Suddenly a shot rang out, then another and another. Bullets were cracking against the outside walls. Freddie threw himself down as people cried out in fear. A sharp smell of burning invaded the building.

"This way," shouted a man, holding open a door behind the counter. "We can get out through the back way. Run!"

Freddie found himself squeezed among the customers and workers crowded around the door. People began to panic. A woman next to Freddie screamed.

There was another burst of gunfire and shouting outside. The woman screamed again.

"Calm down," said Freddie to the woman, wiping the sweat off his forehead. "Breathe slowly." The crowd pushed forward, and Freddie couldn't fight off the panic. His eyes closed. He was unconscious.

The next thing Freddie knew, he was outside in a narrow

alley behind the building. A man was shouting in his ear and slapping his cheek.

"Wake up," said the voice. "Come on!"

As Freddie became conscious again, the man left him and ran off, following the crowd down an opposite alley. A bullet hit the wall next to Freddie. Men with rifles were up on the roofs.

Freddie scrambled to his feet and ran down the alley, which opened into a wider street. When the gunfire sounded more distant, he stopped and leaned against a wall. He was right in the old quarter now and lost. He followed twists and turns until finally he came into a big square that he knew well. There were columns and cafés on all sides and a fountain[16] in the center.

He ran around the square toward the exit on the north side. But ahead of him were men fighting with fists and knives, so he turned back. More men with rifles were on the west side, aiming at a group of fighters in red and black colors just behind him. He turned again and nearly fell over someone lying on the pavement. A boy of about 16. He wore a scarf over his face, but his eyes were frightened. There was blood on his shirt on his right side.

Freddie crouched down next to the boy.

"Can you stand?" he asked in Spanish.

The boy nodded. Freddie helped him to his feet and took his arm. They were beside a door to some apartments. Freddie tried the door and it opened.

"This way," said Freddie, pulling the boy through the door. Freddie helped the boy up the stairs to the top of the building and through a door onto a roof terrace. They found a hiding place and collapsed behind it. Gunfire cracked across the city, and bombs exploded in nearby streets.

"Is it the Nationalists?" said the boy.

"No," said Freddie. "This is insane and crazy. It's one group of Republicans against another. A civil war within a civil war. If you

want to lose a war, fight against your own side. Now, where's this blood coming from?"

The boy pulled up his shirt a little. There was a bullet wound just below his stomach. Freddie looked at the wound and then he looked more closely at the boy. The boy pulled the scarf from his face.

"You're a girl!" Freddie said.

"My name's Laura," she said weakly. "You're not Spanish, are you?"

"I'm from England," said Freddie. He folded Laura's scarf to make a bandage.

"I'm half-English," said Laura in perfect English. "My mother was from London. But I've never been there. I'd like to go one day."

"Let's tie this around the wound to stop the bleeding."

Laura's eyes were beginning to close, and Freddie let her rest.

Some time later, the fighting died down. Freddie helped Laura back down the stairs. He opened the door to the street and cautiously put his head out. The big square was empty.

He only knew one hospital, and it was too far for Laura to walk. They kept close to the wall and moved slowly through the silent streets. Some anarchists with guns challenged them, but Freddie persuaded the men to leave them alone. By the time they reached his building, Laura was struggling to walk.

She carefully washed her wound in Freddie's room, while he made a new bandage.

"What happened?" asked Freddie.

"I was trying to get away from the shooting when I felt this sharp pain," said Laura. "I think a bullet touched my side."

Freddie heated some water and made her a cup of tea.

"We always drank tea at home," she said. "After my mother died, my father tried to carry on some of our English habits." Before she could drink a single mouthful, Laura was fast asleep.

Freddie took the tea and a candle out to the corridor and sat down outside the door. He was angry at himself for fainting at the post office. But then he thought about getting Laura back to his room. His dad would have been proud of him tonight.

Freddie kept watch over Laura until dawn. Then he woke her up.

"We're going to hospital," he said. "Let's see if you can walk."

"I'm sure I can. I'm fine," said Laura. She swung her legs to the ground and stood up.

"Agh!" she cried, sitting back down. "Agh! I think I may need some help."

Gunfire was cracking around the streets. There were men with rifles on the roof of a movie theater, taking shots at anyone on the Ramblas, and all the shops were closed. They made their way north of the main square. By contrast, life here seemed to be continuing as normal. One woman was taking her dog for a walk. The newspaper stands were opening up. There were lines for olive oil, bread, and coffee. They took a bus to the hospital.

There were no empty seats at the hospital. Freddie and Laura sat on the floor in the reception area, under the high curved ceiling. The front line was a long way from here, and only soldiers with very serious injuries were sent back to the city. Many of the cases were people like Laura, caught in the street fighting. Laura's face was white, and she was in a lot of pain. They told each other their life stories while they waited.

"So after your brother joined the army in Madrid, what did you do?" asked Freddie.

"He bought me a train ticket to Barcelona, but I was too upset to leave," said Laura. "I decided to carry on working with the refugees for a while. But then my money started to run out, and I couldn't afford to pay for the room anymore. So I came here."

"And on your first day, you get shot. Welcome to Barcelona!" said Freddie. "Do you know anyone here?"

"My father knows – knew – a lot of people here," explained Laura. "I hoped one of his friends would offer me a room."

Laura changed her position. "Agh!" she said.

"Laura Marcos," called a nurse at last. Laura was taken into a women's ward. Freddie waited outside.

Two hours later, he was still there. Nurses and doctors came in and out of the swinging doors, but nobody spoke to him. Finally, he stopped a young nurse with a friendly face.

"Excuse me," he said, "is there any news of Laura Marcos? They took her in there about two hours ago."

"I'll find out for you," she said, smiling.

Ten minutes later, she came back. Her smile had gone. "She's lost a lot of blood. They're preparing her for an operation now," said the nurse. "Come back tomorrow."

"Is she going to be all right?" asked Freddie.

"Please come back tomorrow," she said and disappeared through the swinging doors.

Chapter 8

Just write!

Barcelona, July 1937

Freddie looked at his reflection in a shop window. There were strips of tape across the glass in case of bombs, but they didn't hide his appearance. He'd been in this city nearly a year, and he'd changed. The city had changed, too, but in the last two months, since those street fights in May. The fighting was over, but the atmosphere was poisonous. The Communists were in charge, and people were being thrown in prison for no reason.

Freddie's once blond hair was darker now, it was much too long, and he really needed a shave. With his red bandana[17] tied around his neck, he looked like a real street fighter. He actually liked the look but decided he'd better clean himself up. Checking the few pesetas in his pocket, he went into the next barber's he came to.

There were two chairs, and one was occupied. Freddie sat in the empty chair. He looked at the man next to him in the mirror – a tall, dark man with a hollow face and piercing eyes[18]. The smell of living rough came off his clothes. He looked at Freddie and gave him a half smile.

The barber put a towel around the man.

"What can I do for you, sir?" he asked.

"Just a shave," said the man. His voice was a whisper, and his Spanish was terrible. He pointed to a wound in his neck. "Take care, please," he said.

Someone called the barber out into the street for a moment.

"Where are you from?" Freddie asked in Spanish.

"England," whispered the man.

"Me, too," said Freddie, in English. "I'm from a mining town near Leeds."

"I know Leeds well," smiled the man. "Are you joining the International Brigades?"

"I'm a message boy for the press office," said Freddie. "I run around for the British and American newsmen. But not for much longer."

"Why not?"

"I'm waiting for a friend to leave hospital. She was shot in the side, and then the wound went bad. So they've kept her there. It's been two months now. But as soon as she's better, we might . . . go to the front."

"To fight?"

"I'd like to try writing some news stories – send them to an English paper."

"Where will you go?"

"Aragon, maybe. It looks like the fighting's about to start there."

"That's where I was wounded. But there's plenty to write about here in Barcelona, while you're waiting," said the man. "Good men are in prison here because they belong to the wrong political party."

The barber came back in, and the man signaled to Freddie to stop talking.

Soon after, Freddie and the man left the shop.

"Have you had any of your stories printed yet?"

"I haven't sent any," said Freddie. "I'm afraid they won't be good enough."

"If you want to be a writer, you have to write," laughed the man. "Just write! You'll get a real buzz the first time you see your name in the paper, and you'll be over the moon when you get your first check."

"What happened to you?" asked Freddie.

"I was shot through the throat," said the man. "Stupid, really. It was early in the morning, and the light was behind me. I stood up and made myself the perfect target. The Nationalist rifleman just had to pull the trigger."

A group of armed men were walking along the street toward them.

"What do you do back in England?" asked Freddie.

"I'm a writer," the man said, but he wasn't listening to Freddie now; he was looking at the guards. "I don't want those men to stop me, so I'm going to disappear." He smiled at Freddie, shook his hand, and crossed the road, melting into a busy alley.

Freddie reached the hospital and waited outside. He hadn't really looked at the hospital building before. It was like a palace from a fairy tale, covered in statues and colored bricks, with rounded and pointed roofs. There was nothing like it in Leeds.

Finally, Laura came through the doors. She shook hands with a nurse and then kissed her. She waved to Freddie, and he ran toward her.

"Hi," he said.

"Hi," she said.

There was an awkward silence.

"Thank you for saving my life, Freddie," she said. "You've been so kind visiting me every day. The nurse said you even came when I was screaming like a madwoman from the fever."

"Oh, well . . . I'm glad you're better. I've brought your bag," said Freddie, holding up the little backpack that Laura had had since she left Badajoz. "I didn't bring it to the hospital – I thought someone might steal it."

"Oh," said Laura, "thanks."

"I didn't know if . . . you know . . . you're going to try and find your father's friends . . . or . . . you might need it," Freddie ran out of words.

"Well, yes, I could try to find someone . . ." said Laura.

"Unless you want to stay, you know, with me?" said Freddie.

"I think there's another room empty on the same floor. Someone just left last week, and it's very cheap."

"Perfect," said Laura.

"Great! Anyway, you're free," said Freddie. "Let's get away from the white coats."

They walked through the hospital gardens. There might be a war, but someone was still looking after the flowerbeds. The colors of the roses sang in the bright July light.

They bought newspapers and sat down at a café table in the sun. After a while, Freddie noticed that tears were running down Laura's face.

"What's wrong?" he said.

"Look at this painting of Guernica – after the Nazi bombs," she said. "There's too much pain."

Freddie studied the painting.

PICASSO'S *GUERNICA* ON DISPLAY IN PARIS

"It's kind of difficult to understand. It's just chaos."

"Look – here is the bull, here is the horse – these are symbols of Spain. Spain is tearing herself apart."

"Who painted it?" asked Freddie.

"Here's a photo of the artist – his name is Picasso. Have you heard of him?"

Freddie looked at the photo and smiled. "Oh! Picasso, yes! I met him – when I was in Paris – he drew a picture of me. I'd never heard of him before."

"You met him?" said Laura, smiling now. "You're joking!"

"I sent his drawing home to my mum," said Freddie. "I hope my dad didn't see it – he would have put it on the fire."

"Did Picasso sign it?" she asked.

"Yes, he did. He was nice – he bought me lunch."

"That's an amazing story," said Laura. "Can I write it and send it to Picasso in Paris, and maybe he can get it published? It might encourage people in France to support the Republic. What do you think?"

"Yeah, OK," said Freddie. "Maybe I'll write it, too, and send mine to an English newspaper."

"Can we use the typewriters in your office?" asked Laura.

"Er, yeah, if they're not being used," said Freddie.

"Come on, then," said Laura. "Let's go. I've wasted two months in that hospital!"

Laura asked Freddie questions all the way to the office, getting every detail of his meeting. By the time they got to a desk, she had planned her opening paragraph.

Freddie introduced Laura to Frank. She told him about Badajoz and about Alonso fighting for the Republic.

"You've got a good personal story to tell there," said Frank. "Why don't you write it up?"

"Hey!" said Freddie. "I've been here for months, and you haven't asked me to write a story."

"I'm waiting for you to insist, Freddie," said Frank. "You've got to be brave – push yourself forward."

Freddie went straight to a free typewriter and put a clean sheet of paper in it. He took off his cap and started typing.

After they had both written their stories, Laura wanted to go to the post office. She thought there might be some letters from her brother waiting for her.

"OK," said Freddie. "Let's get Frank to check our stories and then go down there."

Frank read through the stories quickly. He wrote in pencil all over Laura's article, but he hardly changed a word of Freddie's. It was lunchtime, and the streets were full.

"You know, we talked about reporting from the front when I was in hospital," said Laura, as she and Freddie walked to the post office. "I think we should do it, and then I can find Alonso at the same time."

"You said 'we,'" said Freddie.

"I thought you wanted to go," said Laura. "Couldn't we go together?"

"Yes, great," said Freddie. "I was just . . . yeah, great! I'd love to go with you."

He suddenly grabbed Laura's arm.

"Come over here," he said.

A photographer had set up in the street.

"Let's get our photo taken," said Freddie.

They looked at the photos on display. Most people looked stiff and formal.

"They look like they're about to be shot," laughed Laura. "You know, I'd love to be a photographer. Maybe I'll buy a secondhand camera to take to the front."

"We'll make a perfect team," said Freddie. "You can take the pictures, and I'll write the words."

Freddie and Laura stood together in front of the flower stand next door. They were both laughing when the camera flashed and banged. A passer-by screamed, thinking it was gunfire.

"Come back tomorrow," said the photographer. "One o'clock – your pictures will be ready."

"I'll send a copy to Alonso," said Laura, and they walked on to the post office.

Freddie waited outside. He sat on a bench overlooking the docks, watching a catch of fish being unloaded for the market. Seagulls screamed overhead, looking for fish heads and tails, but there was nothing for them. The fishermen weren't throwing anything away.

Laura reappeared, holding up three letters. She tore them open.

"What's the news?" said Freddie.

"He's fine! He just writes about his daily life and all the things he misses, like coffee and fresh bread," said Laura, quickly reading through the letters. "He might be killed at any minute, and he's sending me a shopping list!"

"That's the best kind of news," said Freddie. "Where is he?"

"He says his unit has joined up with one of the International Brigades near Guadalajara," she said.

It took Freddie and Laura six weeks to persuade Frank. Laura tried all her charm, and Freddie reminded Frank of all the things he had done for him. Finally, Frank produced official permits for them, giving them authority to go to the front on behalf of the Commissariat of Propaganda[19], English-language section.

"I may regret this," said Frank. "Don't get into any trouble."

Chapter 9

Quick thinking!

The front line at Guadalajara, September 1937

"Look at the sky," said Freddie.

"What are they?" asked Laura.

"Shooting stars," said Freddie.

"They're beautiful," said Laura.

They had hitched a ride in the back of an open truck taking medical supplies to the front. Every few meters, they were thrown into the air as the truck hit another hole in the road. The nearer they got to the front, the harder it was to travel. In some places, the roads were completely destroyed.

The truck stopped first at the British section of the International Brigade. They showed their press papers to an officer and got permission to visit the front line.

Laura took photos with the camera she had bought in Barcelona. Freddie made notes. "*Conditions terrible,*" he wrote. "*Trenches full of rubbish. Men desperate about state of guns, lack of cigarettes, disgusting food. Everything running short, except rats and lice[20], the soldiers tell me.*"

Later, they moved on to Alonso's unit. They spoke to one of the officers and interviewed some of the soldiers. Alonso had fought at the Battle of Guadalajara back in March, where the Republicans pushed the Italian unit fighting for Franco right back. It was a famous victory, said the officer.

"My brother is with your unit," said Laura.

"What's his name?" asked the officer.

"Alonso Marcos," she said.

"Ah," said the officer. "One of our best men. He was very brave at Guadalajara."

"Can I see him?" asked Laura.

"He's out on a mission," said the officer.

"When will he be back?" asked Laura.

"Possibly this afternoon," said the officer. "But I'm afraid you can't wait here."

"We'll be back at the medical station," said Freddie. "We can help out while we wait."

There weren't many wounded in the medical station. The fighting over the summer had been mainly up in the north and at Brunete, west of Madrid, and the serious cases were sent back to Valencia or Saragossa. But there was still work to do. The nurses asked Laura and Freddie to help collect firewood and pile it in a barn next to the main building. It was nearly October, and cold weather was on its way.

Laura and Freddie had lunch with the nurses.

"I can see why the soldiers are obsessed with food," said Laura, finishing her soup.

"What *is* this meant to be? It's like river water," said Freddie.

"Laura!" called a voice suddenly.

Laura's soup bowl crashed to the ground as she jumped up and ran to the door. It was Alonso. They hadn't seen each other for nine months, and Laura fell into her brother's arms.

"This is Freddie," said Laura, when she got her voice back.

"Ah! The English boy in the picture," smiled Alonso, stepping forward to hug Freddie. "You saved Laura's life. I can never thank you enough."

"He was amazing," said Laura. "But, Alonso, you look so different," said Laura. She stood back and looked at him carefully.

"I haven't shaved, I haven't had my hair cut, I haven't changed my clothes for weeks," said Alonso, "maybe that's it."

"No, that was all true the last time I saw you," Laura said and stared at him. "It's your eyes . . . they're harder."

Later, they went back to Alonso's headquarters in an empty village. One house still had half a roof and a chimney, and they sat in there around a little fire with an officer and some other soldiers.

"Won't the enemy see the smoke?" asked Freddie.

"We're out of range of their guns," said Alonso.

"Where were you, Alonso, by the way?" said Laura.

"I can't tell you, Laura," said Alonso. "Not even you."

"It's impossible to trust anyone," said the officer. "People have been betrayed on both sides. You never know if the person next to you is waiting to cross over to the other side. We think Alonso is our bravest soldier, but is he really? He could be a Nationalist in disguise!" Everyone laughed.

"So, Freddie, you're a journalist?" said Alonso.

"Well, kind of –" Freddie started to say.

"Of course he is," said Laura, interrupting and pulling some papers and photos out of her pocket.

"He's just being modest. Here's a copy of one of his articles, and here are some of my photos – I took them to go with a story on Republican women in Barcelona."

"Wow!" said Alonso. "I'm impressed. These photos are great!"

"Yes," said Freddie. "She's got a really good eye."

"I've already learned a lot about photography at the press office in Barcelona," said Laura.

As she handed Alonso some more photos, some other bits of paper fell out.

"Let me help," said the officer, picking them up. Alonso saw the letter at once. Laura saw it, too. It was the letter from their brother, Esteban, a lieutenant colonel in Franco's army.

"This one looks official," said the officer, holding Esteban's letter up.

"Actually, no," said Laura, grabbing it. She made it into a ball and threw it toward the fire in one movement. Alonso picked up a stick and pushed it into the center of the flames. The flames briefly burned brightly.

"It's from an old boyfriend," she laughed. "I didn't realize I still had it."

"No need to throw it in the fire!" said the officer.

"No, you're right," said Laura. "But I didn't want Freddie to see it. He might be jealous!"

Later, Alonso walked back to the medical station with Freddie and Laura.

"Well done putting the letter in the fire, Laura," said Alonso. "That was a dangerous moment."

"I couldn't believe I had it with me," said Laura.

"I'd better get back to camp," said Alonso. "How long are you staying at the medical station?"

"We don't know yet," said Freddie. "The doctors can really use our help, so we'll probably stay a few more days. It's giving us great material for stories, too. We'll let you know what our plans are."

Alonso left them, and they walked on in silence.

"That letter," said Freddie, after a few minutes. "Who was it from?"

"Oh," said Laura, "It was from Esteban, our older brother, who's in Franco's army. It said he was our brother and not to harm us."

"So it wasn't from an old boyfriend," said Freddie.

"No," said Laura.

"And you didn't want to hide it from me," he said.

"No," said Laura. "I wanted to hide it from the soldiers. I didn't want to get Alonso into trouble. Or me."

"Right," said Freddie. "Quick thinking!"

"Thanks," said Laura. But then she looked at Freddie. "Oh," she said, "Did you think –"

"No, of course not," said Freddie quickly. "We're mates, you and I – good mates."

*   *   *

There was plenty of work for them at the medical station the next day. The American section of the International Brigades had been involved in some fighting. Several wounded soldiers were brought in, and Laura and Freddie were put to work immediately. Freddie was assisting the only doctor, who was doing emergency operations. Laura was helping the nurses with the patients recovering after the operations.

In the middle of the day, Freddie and Laura went outside for a break. They watched an American ambulance arrive with more casualties. Two soldiers jumped out of the back and carried the injured men into the hospital. Then they came out to look for coffee.

"Well, well, well!" said one of the soldiers. He walked over to Freddie.

"Hey!" said Freddie, and he shook the man's hand. It was Ray.

"Look at you," said Ray. "The boy becomes a man."

"This is Ray," said Freddie to Laura. "My American friend from Barcelona."

"Pleased to meet you," said Laura. "I've heard all about you."

Ray flashed a smile at her. At once, Freddie saw Ray through Laura's eyes. Ray was sophisticated. He had a stylish haircut, perfect teeth, and a great tan.

They exchanged news until the ambulance was ready to leave.

"Are you part of the medical team?" asked Freddie.

"No, I'm just helping out moving the injured. We'll be back tomorrow with the next bunch," said Ray. "We can catch up some more then."

"Sure," said Freddie. "We'll be here."

As Freddie was speaking, they heard a plane screaming overhead, and everyone looked up.

"Enemy plane on fire," someone shouted. "It's coming down."

As flames poured from the engine, a small figure jumped out and fell toward the earth. A parachute opened behind him and pulled him back. The empty burning plane continued to fly, soon disappearing into some trees nearby. Flames and black smoke blew up into the sky. Ray was running before the pilot hit the ground, about 100 meters away from the medical station. The pilot ran as he landed, undoing the parachute without stopping. The ground was uneven, though, with stones and holes, and running was difficult. Ray closed in on the man.

"Stop!" Ray shouted.

The man suddenly turned. He had a pistol and fired at Ray, but his shot was wild. He went on running. Ray speeded up and grabbed him by the legs. Another shot went off as the pilot fell to the ground. The pilot screamed. He had shot himself in the leg.

Freddie was close behind, and he grabbed the pilot's pistol.

"Who do we have here?" Ray said to his prisoner.

Laura came running up to them.

"That was impressive," she said to Ray, her eyes shining. "I've never seen anyone run so fast." Freddie watched her face. He tried to ignore a tiny feeling of jealousy.

The pilot was German and didn't understand Spanish. Alonso and some other soldiers from his unit arrived in a truck and took charge of the prisoner. Freddie introduced Ray to Alonso. The two men chatted for a moment, and Freddie and Alonso carried the prisoner back to the medical station. Ray said good-bye and drove off with the ambulance.

"Does anyone speak German?" asked Alonso. Nobody did.

"Maybe he speaks English," said Freddie.

He sat next to the prisoner and asked him questions in English. "Let's see. Where do you come from? Have you been to London? Do you have any children?" The man didn't answer or show that he understood.

Freddie talked about the Olympic Games. "What did you

think of Jesse Owens? Imagine that – four gold medals at one Olympic Games! What was it now? The 100 m, 200 m, long jump and . . . I can't remember the fourth."

The man didn't move a muscle.

"OK," said Freddie. "I give up."

He stood up and saluted[21]. "Thank you for your time, Lieutenant."

"Captain," said the man, correcting him.

"Oops!" said Alonso. "I think we have an English speaker. See what you can find out while he's being treated, Freddie. I'll question him later."

They carried the prisoner into the medical station, and Alonso waited outside. The doctor gave the prisoner painkillers and prepared to operate. Freddie stayed beside the prisoner while the doctor removed the bullet. The painkillers loosened the prisoner's tongue.

After the operation, Freddie spoke to Alonso and Laura.

"He didn't say much – he talked about some big-name colonel visiting the Nationalist troops at the front just near here – our prisoner was supposed to be there, too. That's about it."

"Did he mention the colonel's name?" asked Alonso.

"Er . . . I think it was Yagüe," said Freddie.

"Colonel Yagüe!" said Alonso and Laura together.

"Who's he?" asked Freddie.

"He led the Nationalist attack on Badajoz," said Laura.

"He marched half the town into the bullring," said Alonso "and then ordered his men to shoot them."

"Can we get him?" said Laura.

"What do you mean?" said Freddie. "You don't mean kill him!"

"I'm thinking," said Alonso. "Last week, while you were waiting for me, I was on a secret mission – behind enemy lines."

"Alonso!" said Laura. "You could have been killed."

"We've got people on the other side," he said. "They help us.

I've been three times. Yagüe will have lots of guards with him, but they won't be expecting an attack."

"You're crazy," said Freddie.

"*I'm* not crazy," said Alonso. "War is crazy."

"Tell your commander," said Freddie. "Get the exact time and place and send a plane over."

"I think we've got more of a chance if we go ourselves," said Alonso. "And anyway, this is personal. Right now, I have to get back to camp, but I'll try to find out more information about Yagüe's visit and make a plan. And don't breathe a word of this."

The medical station was very busy that day, and Freddie and Laura worked without stopping. The American ambulance turned up again the next morning. Freddie helped Ray carry more injured soldiers into the main building.

"Where's the lovely Laura?" asked Ray.

"She's helping the nurses," said Freddie.

"Pretty girl, Freddie. Is she your girlfriend?" asked Ray.

"Not exactly," said Freddie.

"Good," said Ray. "I think I've got a good chance with her. I liked the way she looked at me yesterday."

"Ray, that doesn't mean I don't like her," said Freddie. "Just keep away from her, will you? What kind of man are you?"

"The kind that girls can't resist," laughed Ray.

LOOKING BACK

●●

1 Check your answer to *Looking forward* on page 65.

ACTIVITIES

●●

2 Check (✓) the correct sentence in each pair about Chapter 7.

1 a Journalists are shocked by the destruction of Guernica. ☐
  b Everyone has gotten used to the violence of the civil war. ☐

2 a Freddie acts calmly after the shots in the post office. ☐
  b Freddie panics in the post office and falls unconscious. ☐

3 a The Communists and Anarchists are on the Republican side. ☐
  b The Communists are Republicans and the Anarchists are Nationalists. ☐

4 a Freddie faints when he sees Laura's blood. ☐
  b Freddie gets Laura to safety. ☐

5 a Laura's wound is worse than they thought. ☐
  b The nurse says Laura can go home in two hours' time. ☐

3 Copy words from the text in Chapter 8 that show these facts are true.

1 The street fighting has left bad feelings in the city. (page 74)

....

2 Freddie impresses Laura with his story about Picasso. (page 77)

....

3 Freddie and Laura decide to go to the front. (page 79)

....

4 At first, Frank doesn't want Freddie and Laura to go. (page 80)

....

4 Complete the sentences with the words in the box.

hardships	cigarettes	cold weather	fighting unit
front line	medical station	rubbish and rats	trenches

I am reporting from a ^{1}............................ behind the
^{2}............................ near the Spanish town of Guadalajara. Today,
I was able to visit a Republican ^{3}............................ and talk to
some of the men. There isn't much fighting at the moment,
and the men spend most of the day in the ^{4}............................ ,
where the conditions are terrible. With the ^{5}............................
approaching, they'll get even worse. The trenches are full of
^{6}............................ , and the men's clothes are crawling with lice.
"The food is disgusting," one soldier told me, "and we only get
two ^{7}............................ a day." Despite these ^{8}............................ ,
the men are keeping their spirits up . . .

5 Answer the questions about Chapter 9.

1 Why does Laura throw the letter from Esteban in the fire?

....

2 Why is Ray at the medical station?

....

3 What does Freddie find out from the pilot?

....

LOOKING FORWARD
• •

6 Check (✓) what you think happens in the final chapters.

1 Alonso kills Colonel Yagüe. ☐
2 Laura falls in love with Ray. ☐
3 Freddie asks Laura to marry him. ☐

Chapter 10

It's a private mission

Between two armies, October 1937

"I like a challenge," said Ray.

"Great!" said Alonso, shaking Ray's hand. "You're in." Alonso's plan was simple. He had found out the exact date and time of Colonel Yagüe's visit to the Nationalist camp just two kilometers away. The cook there was a Republican spy, and he had passed information to Alonso before. Colonel Yagüe, the cook said, was going to make a speech to the soldiers on the training ground. Then the Colonel was going to eat a grand meal with the officers, which the cook was already planning. Alonso's idea was to creep up to an isolated group of trees about half a kilometer from the Nationalist camp in the dark and shoot Colonel Yagüe while he was speaking.

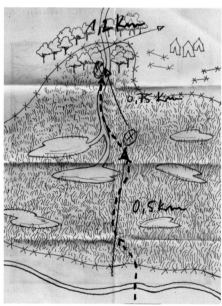

"There's a huge swamp, where there's a break in the front line," Alonso explained. He showed them a map he had drawn.

"There hasn't been much rain this year, and the swamp is dry enough to cross on foot in a couple of places. Here's the idea. We walk past the swamp in daylight as if we're going on to the next section of the front line. Halfway along, we leave the road and hide in the swamp grasses. When it's dark, we all start to crawl across the swamp on our stomachs. Further on, there's a route along a waterway to a group of trees close to the enemy camp. I've used it before, so I know it. We should get a good view of Yagüe from there. And if anyone tries to chase us back across the swamp without knowing the route, they'll sink up to their thighs in mud."

Later, Freddie took Alonso aside and spoke quietly to him.

"I don't know Ray very well," said Freddie. "I don't know if we can trust him on a mission like this."

"I like him," said Alonso. "Look at how he captured that German pilot. I'm not so sure about you, though, Freddie."

"What do you mean?" asked Freddie, surprised.

"Ray told me about your adventure on the train to Barcelona. He says you can't handle danger."

"OK, that happened then, but it wouldn't happen now," said Freddie. "Were you such a great soldier a year ago? Think about it. You've grown up in the last year – so have I."

"I can't take any risks on this mission, Freddie," said Alonso. "I want you and Laura to wait halfway across the swamp as lookouts. Ray and I will carry on to the enemy camp."

"What do you want us to do?" asked Freddie, trying to hide his feelings of injustice.

"To signal when it's safe to cross back," explained Alonso. "Don't forget, we're hiding from both sides – it's a private mission – no one knows about it except us four."

"Tell me one thing," said Freddie. "If Ray hadn't turned up, would you have taken me?"

"Yes, I would," said Alonso.

*　　*　　*

Colonel Yagüe's visit was in four days' time. Alonso and Ray both arranged time off from their units. Freddie and Laura went back to Guadalajara to wait. Freddie wrote articles about the medical station and the front line for the *Yorkshire Evening Post* and sent them to Frank. He signed them, *"Freddie Fox, Eyewitness."* Laura interviewed some of the townspeople and took photos of them in their war-torn city.

The day before the mission, they all met up at the medical station.

"What time is Yagüe making his speech?" asked Freddie.

"Eight o'clock in the evening," said Alonso. "It'll be dark, which is good and bad."

"Good because we can escape in the dark," said Ray.

"Bad because if we're unlucky, someone might see the rifle flash," said Alonso. "There'll be one shot each and one only – fired at exactly the same time."

"So no one will see where the shots came from?" said Laura.

"That's the idea," said Ray.

Alonso and Ray spent the rest of the evening cleaning and oiling their rifles. "This rifle's always jamming," complained Alonso. "I try to fire it, and the trigger gets stuck!"

"Remember when you used to go shooting with Father," said Laura. "He wouldn't let me come. I was very jealous of you and Esteban. You were all being men together, and I was left out."

"You got more than your share of attention most of the time, Laura, as the only girl in the family," said Alonso. "I remember those guns, though! I wish I had one of them now. Look at Ray's gun – it's almost new!"

"You know what Americans are like," laughed Ray. "We always have to have the best."

The conditions were perfect the next afternoon, with a dark and cloudy sky. There was nobody around when they reached the swamp at about five in the evening, and all four crossed the first section of swamp, crawling on their stomachs across the wet ground. Halfway across, they found a reasonably dry area where Laura and Freddie were to wait. Alonso and Ray continued through the swamp. Half an hour later, Freddie and Laura heard Alonso's single owl call. One call meant "Everything OK." Two calls meant "Trouble." Three calls meant "Get out of here."

"That's a perfect owl call," whispered Freddie. "They've reached the waterway. It's another half hour's crawl from there to the camp."

Laura called back.

"You can do it, too!" he said.

"Ssh!" said Laura.

They lay flat, with swamp grasses all around them. At about six, there was suddenly a lot of activity on the road. Three Republican tanks drove by, followed by trucks full of soldiers. As darkness fell, so did the rain. They covered themselves with their coats. The time passed slowly.

"What time is it?" said Laura.

Freddie peered at his watch. "Nearly eight o'clock."

"Yagüe should be making his speech now."

"What's that?" asked Freddie. "Can you hear that? Is it shouting?"

"I can't make it out," said Laura. "It could be coming from the Nationalist camp."

The rain fell more heavily, drowning out any distant sounds.

"This is making me nervous," said Laura. "It's a mad idea. They'll get caught and shot. The enemy will have dogs. Did they think of dogs?"

"Stop worrying," said Freddie. "Alonso's been there before – and the cook would have warned him if there were dogs."

"But if Alonso doesn't come back, that's it – there's only me," said Laura.

"There's your brother, Esteban, and maybe your father is still alive," said Freddie.

"A brother who helped to start this war. I don't know how I would feel if I saw him again," said Laura. "And Father . . . I'm just fooling myself. Of course he was shot in the bullring – I expect they shot him first."

Laura's face was wet from the rain, but Freddie knew she was crying.

"Hey, come on," he said, reaching for her hand. "Let's concentrate on listening for the owl."

Their clothes were wet through, and their bodies began to shake as the cold reached inside them. Still they waited.

"Listen!" said Freddie. The rain was lighter now, and they heard something across the swamp. "Two short calls. That means they're in trouble."

"Oh no!" said Laura.

Then they heard it again – it was definitely two short calls.

"It's them," said Laura.

"Alonso must be alive – he's making the call," said Freddie.

Laura called back to Alonso, and then she and Freddie started to crawl across the ground.

"I think we can run if we keep down low," said Freddie. "We'll get there much faster."

"We must go carefully – we don't want to drown in the swamp."

They stopped to listen every five minutes. The calls were getting louder each time, guiding them. It took them about forty minutes to reach Alonso.

"What's up?" whispered Freddie. "Ray, what's wrong?"

"I've hurt my ankle," said Ray. "Twisted it, I think."

"He's struggling to walk," said Alonso. "It's taken us ages to get back here. Why are you both here? Nobody can tell us if the road is clear."

"I'll go back ahead," said Laura. "I wanted to see you."

"Get going now," hissed Alonso.

Freddie and Alonso dragged Ray back through the swamp. The ground was difficult in the rain. When the road was in sight, they called to Laura. Two calls came back. They waited. A line of trucks came into view, and they lay still in the grass. If anyone saw them appearing out of the swamp now, they would probably shoot them.

Laura called again. One call this time. Everything OK.

When they reached the road, Freddie and Alonso laid Ray on the ground and stood up. Ray's face was white from the pain.

"What happened?" asked Laura, kneeling beside him.

"He jumped down from a tree and fell badly," said Alonso.

"Did you get him?" asked Laura.

"Yagüe?" said Alonso. "No. I could see Yagüe because of his uniform. But we were a long way away. Yagüe moved just as I pulled the trigger, and I hit the man next to him. I saw him go down, and then everyone was running around, shouting. Yagüe ran for the nearest building like a frightened rabbit. But I don't think anybody saw where the shot came from."

"You scared Yagüe, then," said Laura, hugging her brother. "He won't forget that in a hurry. I'm proud of you."

"What about you, Ray?" asked Freddie. "Did you hit anyone?"

"No," groaned Ray. "My gun jammed."

*   *   *

As soon as Freddie appeared in the press office in Barcelona two weeks later, Frank held up two letters for him and one for Laura.

"Where's Laura?" asked Frank.

"A friend of ours got injured in Guadalajara," said Freddie. "She wanted to stay and look after him."

"Who was injured?" Frank asked.

"An American – someone I met when I first came to Spain. He twisted his ankle badly falling out of a tree. Then he caught an infection in the medical station."

"So Laura is staying with him because . . ." Frank invited Freddie to finish his sentence.

"You'll have to ask Laura," said Freddie.

Frank looked at Freddie, waiting for him to say more.

"What!" said Freddie. "Laura and I are just friends, Frank. There's nothing between us."

"When's she coming back?" asked Frank.

"She's staying there – near her brother," said Freddie, "and I'm going back in a couple of weeks. I can take the letter for her."

Frank handed the letters to him. One was from his mother. *"Dear Freddie,"* it started. *"I couldn't believe it when we opened the* Yorkshire Evening Post *and there was your name! I'm so proud of you and so is your father, although he doesn't say anything. He's cut out your article and he keeps looking at it. He thinks I don't know."*

Yorkshire Evening Post

SPANISH REPUBLIC FIGHTS BACK: EXCLUSIVE FRONT LINE REPORT
by Freddie Fox, Eyewitness

Freddie put the letter away to read later. It glowed there with its precious words. His father was proud of him. He'd waited 18 years to hear that. Suddenly he felt a long way from his family.

"I never thought I'd miss them, Frank," he said. "But I do."

"Families look OK from a distance," laughed Frank. "They're not always so good up close!"

The other letter was from the *Yorkshire Evening Post*. Freddie opened it. "*Great stories, Freddie. Keep it up!*" wrote the editor. "*Cheque sent to your parents as requested.*"

"How do you feel?" asked Frank, laughing.

"Over the moon!" said Freddie.

"Now, I wanted to ask you about a story," said Frank. "I know you were near Guadalajara. We had some news of an attempt to kill Colonel Yagüe – he's an important officer in Franco's army. Did you hear anything about that?"

"I don't think so," lied Freddie. "What happened?"

"Well, we didn't get many details – the news came from a Republican spy in the Nationalist camp headquarters there. Apparently another officer standing next to Yagüe was shot – he was quite high up – a lieutenant colonel. He's got the same name as Laura, actually – Marcos – what was it? Here it is – Esteban Marcos."

Frank looked at Freddie. "You look shocked."

"I'm fine, no, I'm fine," said Freddie. "Was he killed, this Marcos?"

"Just wounded, I think. But, like I say, I don't know if the report was true."

Chapter 11

Happy New Year!

Teruel, Christmas 1937

"My fingers are freezing onto the typewriter keys," said Laura.

"This is even colder than Yorkshire in mid-winter," said Freddie.

Laura and Freddie had just met up again after three weeks apart. They sat in the temporary press office in the hillside town of Teruel, with heavy snow falling outside the window. Freddie had traveled from Barcelona in a crowd of journalists and writers. Laura had moved to Teruel from Guadalajara the week before, following Alonso's unit. The war was centered on Teruel.

That day, the Republican soldiers had pushed through the town, fighting from house to house. They had chased the rebel army out. But really, they couldn't have won the battle without the sub-zero weather. The rebel army planes and tanks were frozen solid and couldn't operate. But only for as long as the temperatures stayed low.

"I've just remembered! I've got a letter here for you," said Freddie. "It came to the press office in Barcelona."

"Oh," said Laura, "Look! It's from the *New York Times*."

"I know," said Freddie. "Imagine getting your first piece in the *New York Times!*"

"Let's see if it's a rejection," said Laura, tearing open the letter. "'*Dear Miss Marcos,*'" she read aloud. "'*We loved your piece about Picasso in Paris, and it appeared in the September 5th edition of our newspaper (check enclosed).*'"

Laura screamed and Freddie hugged her.

New York Times

MEETING PICASSO IN PARIS
by Laura Marcos

"Wait a minute!" she said. "It goes on . . . '*We had many letters from our women readers, who enjoyed your female point of view! It was quite political for the Women's Page.*' What! It was a serious piece!"

She made the letter into a ball and threw it on the floor. Freddie picked it up and smoothed it out.

"I thought men and women were supposed to be equal in America," she said.

"Is that what Ray says?" asked Freddie.

"Yeah," said Laura. "I guess they haven't quite got there yet."

After a pause he said, "So . . . how is Ray?"

"He's better," said Laura. "His ankle healed, and he beat off the infection. His brigade's here – they're based quite close to Alonso's unit, I think."

"And are you and Ray . . ."

Laura looked at Freddie.

"Do you love him?"

Laura looked at the keys of her typewriter.

"No, I don't think I love him," she said. "He's fun to spend time with. He kind of takes you along with him."

"He's a charmer," said Freddie.

"So I noticed," said Laura. "The nurses were around him like butterflies. He enjoyed it, too. But he has asked me to go back to America with him."

"Oh," said Freddie, shocked. "And you said . . ."

"I haven't given him an answer yet," said Laura. "But I think the answer's going to be no. I don't think he's the man for me . . ."

"So are you still seeing him?" asked Freddie.

"No, not really," said Laura.

"Then I think you should come out with me," said Freddie, with a large grin on his face. "Especially as it's Christmas Eve."

Everyone on the Republican side was celebrating. They had defeated Franco's men in most of Teruel, and they felt good for the first time in weeks despite the freezing temperatures. It was -20°C outside, and everyone sat as close to the fires as they could. Freddie and Laura joined some of the British soldiers. They sang Christmas songs and ate chocolates.

Between Christmas and New Year, it snowed heavily every day. There was fighting in the streets in the south of the town. On New Year's Eve, Freddie and Laura followed a Republican unit on a mission to capture the Bank of Spain from the Nationalists. They stayed well back from the fighting, watching from the doorway of an abandoned café. The door to the café was broken down, and everything inside had been taken.

There was a pause in the shooting, and the snow fell silently around them.

"Listen," said Laura. "What's that?"

"What?" asked Freddie.

"Listen," said Laura. "There it is again. I can hear a voice, a child's voice. It's under our feet."

They brushed the snow off the pavement with their feet to reveal wooden doors. They pulled open the doors.

"Hello," called Laura into the darkness. She climbed halfway down a ladder into the dark cellar. There in the corner were two young boys, dirty and thin, with hollow eyes. Laura spoke kindly to them, but they were terrified. When Freddie found some bread in his backpack, they came forward. The snow was falling really thickly now and piling up on the steps behind them, and it was hard to see.

Laura led the boys up the ladder into the street.

"We can't go far in this weather," said Freddie. "I saw a church in the next street. Maybe we can use it as a shelter until the snow stops."

Freddie carried the younger boy, and Laura held the hand of the older boy. The snow blinded them as they ran. The main doors to the church were locked, but they found an open door around the side. Some stones and dust covered the floor and benches inside, but the building wasn't badly damaged.

"We'll have to stay here until the snowstorm stops," said Freddie. "Let's see what we can find."

"These will be warm," said Laura, pulling down some heavy red curtains that closed off a side chapel. They went into the side chapel and made a bed for the boys with the curtains. Freddie found some water.

"I've got some cake in my bag," Freddie said quietly to Laura. "We can give it to the boys later."

A large monument in the center of the side chapel was covered with a blanket. They pulled the blanket off for more bedding, revealing statues of a young woman and man.

"Oh look!" said Laura. "I recognize these two! *Los amantes de Teruel*. The lovers of Teruel. Aren't they beautiful?"

She showed the boys the faces of the two lovers and how they held hands from their graves.

Freddie found a box of matches and lit some church candles. He put the matches in his pocket. As the snow continued to fall outside, hiding the sound of gunfire, Laura told the boys the story of the lovers of Teruel.

"Long ago," she said, "a boy and a girl loved each other very much."

"What were their names?" asked the older boy.

"Diego and Isabel," said Laura. "They were going to marry when they were older, and their parents were very happy. But life was kind to one family and cruel to the other. Isabel's family became rich. Diego's family lost all their money, and they had to wear rags. When Isabel and Diego were 15, Isabel's father said the marriage was off. He wasn't going to join his fine family to a pack of dogs, he said. But Isabel still loved Diego. 'Please, father,' said Isabel, 'I love Diego.' But her father wouldn't change his mind. Then Diego came to see him. 'Sir,' he said, 'I will go into the world and make my fortune. If I return in exactly five years with more money than you have ever seen, can I marry your daughter?'"

The younger boy was fast asleep, and the older one was trying hard to keep his eyes open.

"Isabel's father was moved by the boy's love for his daughter," continued Laura. "He agreed. Five years passed. Isabel was 20 and very beautiful. She sat all day by the window, looking out for Diego. She was sure he would come, but he didn't. Her father had

another man waiting to marry her, and the wedding took place in the morning."

Both boys were now fast asleep.

"Please finish the story," said Freddie.

"Diego arrived the same day on a beautiful white horse. Isabel and her father had counted the day Diego left as the first day of the five years, but Diego hadn't. He asked Isabel to kiss him, but she refused. 'It wouldn't be fair to my husband,' she said. Diego died at once of a broken heart, and his body was brought into the great hall. Isabel told her husband the story. 'Kiss him,' said her husband. She went up to Diego's body and kissed him –"

"Who's there?" called a voice.

"The candles!" hissed Laura.

They put them out and lay still.

"We're soldiers," said the voice. "We can help you."

"Thank goodness," said Laura, standing up.

"No, wait –" whispered Freddie.

"Here," called Laura.

A torch shone into the chapel. Freddie and Laura could make out three soldiers in the light.

"Happy New Year!" said the soldiers, pointing their rifles at Freddie and Laura. They were Franco's men.

*   *   *

The next day, the Nationalist soldiers pushed the prisoners into trucks. It was still snowing hard, and they could hear gunfire and explosions as the battle in Teruel became more intense.

"I don't think they've got time to question or search us," whispered Freddie to Laura as they squeezed into the open trucks.

Laura looked around suddenly. "I heard someone call my name," she said. She looked ahead to the other trucks and caught sight of Ray.

They moved off soon afterward.

"Ray's in one of the other trucks," she whispered to Freddie.

"Is he? Which one?"

"Not the next one, but the one ahead of that, I think," she said.

The trucks left the sounds of battle behind.

"I'm worried about the little boys," said Laura. "I hope they treat them well."

"I'm sure they'll take them somewhere safe," said Freddie.

*　*　*

Two days later, the line of trucks was still bumping along the road.

"Where are they taking us?" said Freddie.

"Way up north somewhere," said Laura. "I don't know why they didn't just shoot us."

"There are prisoners from lots of different countries here," said Freddie. "Maybe they want to see who they've got first."

The trucks were open at the back, and a few prisoners were dying from the cold. Freddie and Laura were in the last truck. A Nationalist soldier with an eye-patch and a rifle stood on the back of the truck, and an armored car with four more soldiers followed behind them. Freddie and Laura held tight to each other, to keep warm and to keep from bouncing out of their seats. As the trucks began to climb up into mountains, they slowed to walking pace. Snow was falling heavily. Suddenly there was a crashing sound up ahead and shouts all along the line.

"What's happened?" shouted one of the soldiers in the armored car behind.

"A truck's in trouble up ahead," said the soldier with the eye-patch. "It's driven over the edge of the road."

"Jump in," shouted the soldier in the armored car.

It pulled out onto the other side of the road, and the soldier with the eye-patch climbed onto it. Then they drove up to the accident. Laura pulled her beret over her ears and tried to close her collar to keep the snow out.

Freddie pulled Laura's sleeve.

"We won't get another chance like this," he hissed. "Come on."

They half climbed half fell out of the side of the truck. They ran across the road, jumped over a low wall, and headed for some trees, slipping and sliding on the snow-covered grass.

Suddenly there was someone right behind them.

"Keep going," he shouted. It was Ray.

As they reached the trees, they heard shouts. Bullets cracked behind them.

They ran through the trees, jumping over roots and ditches. They headed upward, as more shots rang out behind them. They were very high up the mountainside when they stopped running and put their hands in the air.

The soldiers from the armored car had driven around the other way. They stood in front of them with their rifles raised. The ground was uneven here, and the snow was very deep in places. Freddie, Laura, and Ray backed away.

"Hold it!" shouted the soldier with the eye-patch, preparing to fire. They took one more step backward, and suddenly they disappeared through the snow and were falling into darkness, sliding and slipping. And then they hit a wall of earth and stopped moving. Silence. Freddie got onto his knees. A faint light fell from above them, and faint voices came from the same place.

"Quick," said Freddie. "Get on your feet."

"Come on! Move," said Ray.

"What happened?" said Laura.

"We fell down a hole," said Ray. "We must be in a cave or a mine. Let's get away from the hole. They might follow us."

They couldn't see much, but they could just make out a tunnel. They crouched down and half ran. They could feel walls on either side. They moved as fast as they could, covering a lot of ground, but the tunnel began to get narrower.

Kaboom! There was a loud thud behind them and a sudden bright light. A rush of heat came down the tunnel toward them, and they were showered with earth. Laura screamed and Ray cried out.

"Keep moving!" cried Freddie.

"What was that?" asked Laura.

"Some kind of bomb," said Freddie. "That's good – they can't come after us."

"But now we can't get out!" cried Laura.

Chapter 12

We're being buried alive!

Northern Spain, January 1938

First came the sweating and then the shaking. Freddie had managed to get down the tunnel ahead of the others, but now he felt his body beginning to fight him. He breathed as slowly as he could, but his heart was racing.

"You guys, I have to tell you something," Freddie said when he could speak.

"What?" said Laura. Her voice was shaking, too.

"I'm not good underground," he said. "I'm actually finding it quite hard to breathe."

"OK, I don't like it either," said Laura. "What shall we do?"

"Just sit here," said Freddie. "For a minute."

"No, let's keep moving," said Ray. "We need to get out." He was breathing fast and hard as well, and his voice sounded high and tense. "We're being buried alive."

"Suppose there's no way out," said Laura. "Suppose that hole was the only way into these caves. Suppose there are animals in here. What lives in caves? Snakes? Bears?" Laura wiped her forehead.

"Laura," said Freddie. "Calm down."

"Freddie, Ray," she said. "I'm afraid. I'm shaking. I want to get out. We have to find a way out. Now."

They couldn't see each other in the blackness. Then Freddie remembered the matches from the church. He tried to give them to Ray, but Ray's hands were shaking too much. Freddie lit a match and stuck it in the earth wall. He took hold of Laura's face.

"OK, listen to me," Freddie said. "Count with me. One, two, three . . ." They counted twice to ten, first in English, then in Spanish. They breathed together, in rhythm.

They were both silent for a moment, and then Laura spoke.

"Freddie, that didn't help," she said.

When he heard the panic still in her voice, Freddie felt his own fear disappear in response. His mind cleared. He understood what he had to do. He loved this girl, and he had to save her. He was the one who knew about tunnels and mines, and he had to take charge.

"Let's find out where we are," said Freddie. "This tunnel must lead somewhere. Laura, take Ray's hand. Follow me."

They continued along the narrow, uneven tunnel on their hands and knees. Freddie felt they were going down, getting deeper underground, but he kept talking to Laura over his shoulder, concentrating on her.

"Talk to me, Laura," he said. "What happened at the end of the story to the lovers of Teruel? What happened to Isabel?"

"She-she – I don't know," said Laura. "I-I can't remember."

"Maybe she lived happily ever after with her second-best husband?" he said.

"No, that's it, I remember, she died, too. She kissed Diego and she died, like him, of a broken heart."

"Save the fairy tales for later," called Ray from the back. He didn't sound himself.

Freddie stopped.

"We've come to a junction," he said. "Hang on – I'll light another match."

The dancing light revealed two tunnels. One went up to the right, the other down to the left.

"This way," said Freddie, starting off into the left-hand tunnel.

"No, Freddie," said Ray. "You're leading us down. We need to be going up."

The match went out.

"No," said Freddie. "This is right. I can feel the air. It's moving and it's colder. Can you feel it? There's a bigger space up ahead – maybe a bigger tunnel or even a cave."

"No, you're wrong," said Ray. "I'm going the other way. I need oxygen."

"Ray!" said Freddie. "Come this way. I know what I'm talking about. Stay with me."

"Ray!" called Laura. Her breathing was very fast. "Freddie, he let go of my hand. He's gone."

"Ray!" called Freddie. "Come back."

But Ray didn't answer. They heard him disappearing deeper into the mountain.

"OK," said Freddie. "Something's up ahead. Something big."

They crawled along for about 10 minutes until the tunnel became wider and higher. "We can nearly stand up here," said Freddie. "Come on, Laura. I'll go back for Ray."

After another 20 meters, they turned a corner and the tunnel suddenly opened into a large cave. They couldn't see the space, but they could feel it and hear it. Freddie and Laura moved forward, keeping close together, Freddie slightly ahead.

"Oh, thank goodness," said Laura. Her breathing became more normal.

"Ow," said Freddie.

"What is it?" said Laura.

"I've banged into something," he said, feeling forward with his hands. "It's a wooden table. There are lamps here, like miners' lamps."

"Are we in a mine?"

"We must be," said Freddie. "Although the tunnels aren't like any mine tunnels I've ever seen. They feel older, much older."

Freddie lit two of the lamps. They jumped to life.

"I don't believe it," said Laura, holding up her lamp. "I recognize this place. I know exactly where we are. It isn't a mine, and I've been here before."

They still couldn't see the size of the cave. But they could see the walls. They were covered in paintings of bulls, horses, and men with weapons.

"This is Monte Castillo. My father brought us here when I was about 10."

"We need to find a way out of here," said Freddie.

They walked around the edge of the cave and through an opening into a second cave. They had to move carefully to avoid cutting themselves on the sharp rocks.

"I can smell fresh air," said Freddie.

"Freddie, you've saved my life again!" said Laura. "That tunnel was terrifying. And you said *you* hated being underground."

"Actually," said Freddie, "I think you've cured me. Thinking about you stopped me thinking about me. I've hated small, dark spaces all my life. I've been fighting against my fear for years, but now I feel like I've beaten it."

"What about Ray?" said Laura.

"Right," said Freddie. "You stay here, and I'll go back for him. Will you be OK?"

"I'm fine here. Take two lamps in case one goes out."

Freddie made his way back to the tunnel opening in the first cave. Freddie looked at the narrow, dark, damp hole in the lamplight, but he didn't hesitate. He went straight in, falling to his hands and knees as the tunnel narrowed, and followed his way back. At the junction, he turned into the right-hand tunnel going upward.

"Ray!" he called. "Ray!"

Freddie pushed on, a feeling of strength flooding through his body. He wasn't sweating or shaking. He wasn't afraid. He could do this. But where was Ray? The tunnel was getting hotter and narrower as it went deep into the mountain. He held his lamp in front of him as he moved, but stopped suddenly when the tunnel dropped away in front of him. There was a kind of cliff edge. He looked over, but the lamp was too weak to show him more than a couple of meters ahead.

He kept still and listened. He was sure he could hear breathing.

"Ray?" he called. "Is that you?"

After a moment, there was a distant reply – a kind of groan.

"Hang on, mate," said Freddie. "I'm coming."

He leaned forward over the edge and made out a shelf of rock. Climbing down onto it, he saw that the tunnel sloped steeply to the right. Lying on his back, he made his way down the tunnel.

"Agh!" he cried, as his foot sunk into something soft.

"Ow!" came the reply.

"Ray?" said Freddie, holding up his lamp. Ray was lying in a heap, but he was still alive.

"What took you so long?" said Ray, lifting his head from the damp earth and smiling weakly at his rescuer.

"Hey!" said Freddie, smiling broadly. "I thought you might be a bull. We're in prehistoric caves, covered with ancient paintings. It's amazing! Come on, let's get back to Laura."

Ray followed Freddie slowly back to the main cave. His back hurt, and he was still shaking.

"Thanks, buddy," said Ray. "I thought I was going to die back there."

"You're welcome," said Freddie. "If there's one thing I know about, it's tunnels."

"I thought you hated being underground," said Ray.

"So did I," said Freddie. "But I seem to have won that battle today."

"And I wanted to say," said Ray, "about Laura. I know you're in love with her, and I'm sorry I've been getting in your way. She's a great girl, but she spends most of her time talking about you when she's with me."

"Does she?" said Freddie. He couldn't keep the pleasure out of his voice.

At that moment, they arrived at the main cave. Laura had lit a series of lamps along the wall. As the light danced over the delicate paintings of animals and human figures, an ancient world came to life before their eyes. It was very beautiful.

While they waited for nightfall, they hunted around for anything useful, but it seemed like the caves had been closed up for a while. Laura knew roughly where they were, and they decided to head to the French border and cross at the coastal town of Irún. It would probably take them a couple of weeks to get there, and it was through Nationalist territory, but they didn't know what else to do.

"Ready?" said Laura.

"I think so," said Freddie.

"Yup," said Ray.

And out they went.

Chapter 13

Now what do we do?

SPANISH REFUGEES FLOOD BORDER: MANY HELD IN CAMPS

Two weeks later, the three travelers looked down on the busy border town of Irún. Their clothes were in rags. The snow still lay deep across the mountains and hills around them.

The actual border here between France and Spain was a river, and the main crossing point was a wide bridge. They could see across the border to the neighboring town of Hendaye in France. Groups of French guards were patrolling the entrance to Hendaye. They decided not to try and talk their way across. They were sure they would be sent back into Franco's hands.

The travelers now walked east from Irún, following the course of the river, until they came to a ruined farmhouse.

"Now what do we do?" said Freddie.

"We could try swimming across to France after dark," said Laura.

"I can't swim," said Freddie.

The others looked at him and then looked at each other. They couldn't believe it.

"What!" said Freddie. "I've never had a chance to learn."

"Maybe there's something here we can use as a boat," said Ray.

An hour searching in the barns behind the farmhouse produced some wood and broken barrels, which they knocked into a basic boat. They were quite proud of it. It had started to rain hard, and the snow was finally beginning to melt. By the time they got down to the river with their boat, their feet were caked with mud.

They tied the boat to a tree and then pushed it into the water. The river was fairly wide here and very fast as it began its rush to the sea. The river immediately took the boat to the extreme of the rope, pulling at it hard. The noise of the rushing water and the rain was deafening, and they had to shout to be heard.

"Won't it just take us straight round the corner?" said Freddie. "They'll shoot us from the bridge!"

"We must get as close as we can to the other side. We may have to swim the last bit," said Laura.

"Freddie can't swim," said Ray.

"We'll have to rope him to us," said Laura.

"No way!" said Ray. "We'll all drown."

"Maybe if we all row hard, we can get the boat to the opposite bank, or near enough to jump onto the bank," suggested Freddie.

On the other side of the river, an old tree leaned right over the water.

"Let's head for that tree," said Laura. "We'll be OK."

They climbed onto the boat, carrying pieces of wood for rowing.

"Ready?" shouted Laura, and she undid the rope.

The boat shot off to the left. They all rowed like mad on the left side, steering the boat toward the tree. Freddie was at the front as the boat went close to the tree.

"Freddie!" shouted Laura. "Grab the branch!"

Freddie threw down his piece of wood, stood up, and hung on to the branch. Part of the tree was under the water and caught the boat. Laura grabbed the branch next to Freddie. Laura and Freddie both climbed into the tree, but as they stepped off the boat, it broke free again.

"Help!" cried Ray, grabbing a branch as he fell into the water.

Laura crawled back along the branch. Suddenly a shot rang out and cracked off the tree. A border patrol was on the Spanish side of the river. Two border guards were aiming at them with rifles.

"Hurry!" cried Freddie from the bank.

Laura was above Ray now. She lay down flat and held out her hand. Ray grabbed it, as another bullet hit the tree. Laura started to move backward, holding tight to Ray.

"Stay under the water," she shouted to Ray. "Don't give them a target to hit."

The rain was even heavier now, and the guards had to stop to reload their rifles. Laura reached the bank, and she and Freddie dragged Ray out of the water.

Out of sight of the guards, they lay on the bank, in the rain. Cold, wet, exhausted, and starving, but still alive.

*   *   *

After they had hitched a ride to Saint Jean de Luz with a French farmer, Ray went off to find the American consulate to get a new passport and then to see about a ticket to New York, while Freddie and Laura headed for the British consulate. It was a cream building with the windows and doors picked out in red. Plants were starting to climb the walls, their spring flowers ready to explode with color. Laura rang the bell. A woman answered.

"*Oui?*" she said.

"My name is Laura Marcos," Laura answered in English. "I've come from Spain."

"We have so many refugees from Spain," said the woman, closing the door. "Go to the Town Hall, they'll help you there."

"No, no," said Laura. "I have come here because my uncle is the British Consul. He is – was – my mother's brother. Please tell him I'm here – Laura Marcos."

The woman looked carefully at the ragged pair.

"Wait there," said the woman and she closed the door.

Freddie and Laura went down the steps and sat down. They had their backs to the door.

"We made it," said Freddie. "I can't believe we're here."

"We've been to hell and back, Freddie," Laura said, but then the door opened again.

Freddie turned around. He saw an old man.

"Is this your uncle?" asked Freddie.

Laura turned around and jumped up.

"No!" cried Laura, and the tears flowed. "It's my father."

* * *

After much emotion, a hot bath, a change of clothes, and the best meal they had ever eaten, Laura and Freddie sat in a small sitting room with Señor Marcos.

"So Alonso was fighting at Teruel," said Señor Marcos. "I find it hard to imagine."

"You wouldn't recognize him," said Laura. "He's a real action man. His officer said he was the bravest soldier in the unit!"

"He was always the best shot when I took the boys shooting," laughed Señor Marcos, and then he stopped. "That's a strange feeling. Do you know, Laura, I haven't laughed for a year and a half."

"How did you get here, Señor Marcos?" asked Freddie.

"Please call me Javier. I owe you so much, Freddie," said Laura's father. "Well, during the fighting, I was stuck in the house. My ankle was injured in an explosion, and I was useless. Yagüe, the Nationalist commander, took over our house. He was a brutal man. He rounded up thousands of us and marched us into the bullring. They were ready to start shooting us –"

"Oh, Father," said Laura, taking her father's hand. "I tried not to imagine that. How did you escape?"

"Esteban saved me," said Laura's father. "He was Yagüe's right-hand man, but he didn't arrive in Badajoz until the day of the massacre. He saw me in the first line of men and told the soldiers to wait. He came forward and helped me out of the bullring. He put me in a car with letters and an armed guard. They drove me up here to Irún, and your uncle collected me at the border."

"Thank God," said Laura. "But you had no news of us. If we had known you were here, I could have told you we were safe."

"And perhaps you would have come here sooner," said Laura's father.

"Everything changed when we got to Madrid," said Laura. "We realized then that we had to fight. Especially Alonso. He will never give up the fight – he will die first."

"I wonder where Esteban is," said Laura's father. "I haven't heard anything from him, but I expect he's safe. He's on the winning side, after all."

Freddie looked at Señor Marcos with his white hair and sad eyes. He didn't say anything about the shooting of Esteban.

Perhaps the story would come out in the future, but Laura and her father didn't need to hear it now.

"And you, Laura," said her father. "Will you go back?"

"I don't think so, Father. Your hair's already gone white because of this war – I think it would kill you if I left you again."

"What about you, Freddie?" he said. "It's not really your war, after all."

"It is, sir," said Freddie. "This fight against Franco is for freedom and for Europe. We may be losing this battle, but we'll win the next one."

"Yes, I'm afraid it's too late for Spain," said Señor Marcos sadly. "I don't think the Republic can survive now. It looks like Spain will have a dictator with total power – *Generalísimo* Franco."

*   *   *

The next day, Freddie and Laura sat in a café overlooking the harbor.

"You look nervous," said Freddie.

"Oh, there he is," said Laura, jumping up and running across the square.

Freddie watched as they talked for a moment. They came toward the table and sat down. Ray and Freddie shook hands. Two or three big ships sat in the harbor.

"You look so different," said Laura to Ray. "All polished up."

"You look lovely, too," said Ray. "And Freddie, too, of course. I wish you were both coming to New York with me. We've been through a lot together. In fact, now you've both saved my life! And the Big Apple is just over there." He pointed out to sea. "The Statue of Liberty is waiting to greet you."

"I can't wait to see New York," said Laura, turning to Freddie. "Freddie and I will come and visit you as soon as we've saved Europe, won't we?"

*   *   *

MINE BOSS RECOVERS FROM
TWO-YEAR COMA:
Freddie Fox saved my life!

The train pulled into Freddie's hometown. Laura put her head out of the window as the station came into view.

"What's going on?" she said. "It looks like they're expecting someone."

Freddie looked out.

"There must be someone important on the train," he said.

"And it looks like it's you!" said Laura, laughing in amazement.

"*Welcome Home Freddie Fox*," read a homemade flag. And there stood Freddie's mother and father, his brothers and sister, his friends, and half the town, waving and cheering. A photographer's bulb flashed as Freddie and Laura stepped down.

FREDDIE'S WAR OVER FOR NOW

Our man
in Spain
returns
to hero's
welcome!

Beyond Spain

General Franco and the Nationalist rebel army won the Spanish Civil War, finally taking full power on April 1, 1939. Spain did not fight in the Second World War, as it began the long recovery from three years of brutal civil war. Franco ruled Spain as a dictator until his death in 1975.

Alonso was taken prisoner at the great final battle of the Spanish Civil War at the River Ebro in November 1938. He spent the rest of the war in prison, until he was sent to fight for the Germans in the Second World War on the eastern front. He escaped and returned to France, where he helped Spanish refugees to escape to the United States and Britain. When peace came, he joined his father in London. He returned to Spain in 1978 and lived in Madrid until he died at the age of 90.

Ray wasn't back in New York for long. He returned to Europe with the U.S. Army. He was killed on Omaha Beach on June 6, 1944 – D-Day.

Laura became a photojournalist during the Second World War and won prizes for her pictures of the Liberation[22] of Paris in 1944.

Freddie became chief war reporter for a national newspaper. He was present at the D-Day landings and followed the Allied armies[23] into Berlin. After the war, Freddie tried his hand at fiction and became a successful writer.

In 1945, Laura and Freddie married in Yorkshire and moved to London to be near Laura's father. They bought a little house overlooking the River Thames and had three children, living long into old age.

LOOKING BACK

● ●

1 Check your answers to *Looking forward* on page 91.

ACTIVITIES

● ●

2 Complete these sentences about Chapter 10.

1 Alonso gets information about the Nationalist camp from

....

2 Alonso takes Ray on the mission instead of Freddie because

....

3 Freddie and Laura suddenly run to meet Alonso and Ray because

....

4 Alonso didn't shoot Colonel Yagüe. He shot the man

....

5 Alonso actually shot ....

6 Laura hasn't come back to Barcelona with Freddie because

....

3 Put the events from Chapter 11 in order.

1 Freddie and Laura are pushed into trucks with other
   Republican prisoners, including Ray. ☐
2 Freddie and Laura, sing songs and eat chocolates. ☐
3 Freddie, Laura, and Ray jump out and try to escape. ☐
4 The line of trucks stops after an accident. ☐
5 The Nationalist soldiers surround them with guns. ☐
6 They find two terrified children in a cellar. ☐
7 They step back and fall through a hole in the ground. ☐
8 Freddie and Laura are taken prisoner. ☐

4 Underline the correct words in each sentence about Chapter 12.

1 *Freddie feels / They all feel* afraid in the black tunnel.

2 Freddie *takes charge / loses control.*

3 Freddie chooses the *right / wrong* tunnel to follow.

4 Laura *recognizes / has never seen* the Monte Castillo caves.

5 Ray is *awake / unconscious* at the bottom of a steep slope.

6 Ray *is sure / doesn't think* Laura is interested in Freddie.

7 They head *for the French border / back to Barcelona.*

5 Are the sentences about Chapter 13 true (*T*) or false (*F*)?

1 The three travelers cross into France over a bridge at Irún. ☐

2 They decide to swim across the river further down. ☐

3 They manage to row their boat to the opposite bank. ☐

4 French border guards shoot at them from the French side of the river. ☐

5 Laura is reunited with her father at the British consulate. ☐

6 Esteban saved their father from the massacre at Badajoz. ☐

7 Laura decides to go to New York with Ray. ☐

8 Freddie arrives home to a hero's welcome. ☐

Although Freddie's story is not true, it takes place against the background of real people and events. Freddie meets the following real people: Pablo Picasso (pages 27–9), photographers Endre Friedmann (Robert Capa) and Gerda Taro (pages 29–31) and writer George Orwell (pages 74–6). Laura and Alonso meet journalist Jay Allen (pages 36–9) and hear political leader Dolores Ibárruri ("*La Pasionaria*") on the radio (page 45).

GLOSSARY

●●

[1]**democratically** (page 5) *adverb*   based on the wishes or votes of the majority of the people

[2]**fascist** (page 14) *noun*   someone who believes in the superiority of a nation or race, and a political system based on a powerful leader, that is without political or personal freedom

[3]**Consul** (page 19) *noun*   an official chosen by a government to help its citizens in a foreign country

[4]**Communist** (page 22) *noun*   someone who believes in a society in which property is owned by the community as a whole, with emphasis on the needs of the state instead of individual liberties

[5]**straw** (page 24) *noun*   the long, dried thin part of a plant that the leaves and the flowers grow on, which is dried and used as bedding for animals

[6]**garlic** (page 30) *noun*   a vegetable in the onion family, with a very strong taste and smell

[7]**Catholic** (page 38) *adjective*   belonging to the part of the Christian religion whose leader is the Pope in Rome

[8]**Anarchist** (page 39) *noun*   someone who believes that people should directly organize a **socialist** or **communist** society themselves, without political parties or leaders

[9]**checkpoint** (page 39) *noun*   a place where people and vehicles are stopped and examined

[10]**crew** (page 47) *noun*   a team of people with special skills who work together

[11]**freight** (page 48) *noun*   goods, but not passengers, that are carried from one place to another

[12]**Socialist** (page 56) *noun*   someone who believes in a society in which property is owned by the community as a whole

[13]**barricade** (page 57) *noun*   something that is put across a road to stop people from going where they want to go

[14]**stew** (page 61) *noun*   food made of vegetables and meat cooked slowly in liquid

[15]**sardine** (page 66) *noun*   a small sea fish that can be eaten

[16]**fountain** (page 69) *noun*   a decorative structure in a lake or a pool that forces water up into the air

[17]**bandana** (page 74) *noun*   a brightly colored piece of cloth that is worn around the neck or head

[18]**piercing eyes** (page 74) *noun*   used to describe a person looking very carefully at someone or something, especially when they are trying to discover something

[19]**Commissariat of Propaganda** (page 80) *noun*   a Republican department created during the civil war to spread culture and information

[20]**lice** (page 81) *noun*   plural of louse, a small insect that lives in people's clothes or hair, or in animals' fur or on their bodies

[21]**salute** (page 88) *verb*   to give a formal sign of respect to someone, especially by raising the right hand to the side of the head

[22]**liberation** (page 123) *noun*   when something or someone is released or made free

[23]**Allied armies** (page 123) *noun*   the armies from countries, including the United States, the U.K., the U.S.S.R., and France, that agreed to help each other during the Second World War